# Digital
# Rush

# Digital Rush

## Nine Internet Start-Ups in the Race for Dot-Com Riches

### Jonathan R. Aspatore

with
**Alicia Abell**

AMACOM
American Management Association

New York • Atlanta • Boston • Chicago • Kansas City • San Francisco • Washington, D.C.
Brussels • Mexico City • Tokyo • Toronto

Special discounts on bulk quantities of AMACOM books are available to corporations, professional associations, and other organizations. For details, contact Special Sales Department, AMACOM, a division of American Management Association, 1601 Broadway, New York, NY 10019.
Tel.: 212-903-8316. Fax: 212-903-8083.
Web site: www.amacombooks.org

This publication is designed to provide accurate and authoritative information in regard to the subject matter covered. It is sold with the understanding that the publisher is not engaged in rendering legal, accounting, or other professional service. If legal advice or other expert assistance is required, the services of a competent professional person should be sought.

Library of Congress Cataloging-in-Publication Data

Aspatore, Jonathan Reed.
    Digital rush : nine internet startups in the race for dot.com riches / Jonathan R. Aspatore ; with Alicia Abell.
      p.  cm.
    Includes index.
    ISBN 0-8144-0567-3
    1. Electronic commerce—Case studies.   2. Electronic commerce—Management—Case studies.   3. New business enterprises—Management—Case studies.   4. New business enterprises—Computer networks—Case studies.   5. Internet.   I. Abell, Alicia, 1973– II. Title.
    HF5548.32.A836 ~~2000~~ 2001
    658.8'4—dc21                                  00-044800

Printing number

10  9  8  7  6  5  4  3  2  1

For all those
that ever had the courage to pursue a dream.

# Contents

# Preface

Starting and managing a successful Internet business involves the right combination of skills, hard work, and luck. There is no set formula for achieving success as an Internet entrepreneur. Each successful Internet entrepreneur has taken a different path and created his or her own unique strategies and insights regarding what it takes to succeed. By sharing the experiences, ideas, and strategies of some of the most interesting Internet entrepreneurs of our time, *Digital Rush* aims to help individuals with an online dream to create their own "virtual reality."

Although little formal training can prepare you to start an Internet business, one of the best ways to learn is through the stories of other successful Internet entrepreneurs. Each of the people interviewed in this book has had a different path to success. All encountered numerous roadblocks and various struggles on their way to fulfilling their visions for their businesses. They all persevered by identifying and exploiting the right combination of people and resources and marrying those strengths with an unrelenting desire to succeed.

The time to be a part of an online venture is now. First, online advertising dollars are at all-time high, and

Internet connection times have never been faster (with broadband capabilities waiting round the corner). The international community's adoption rate is predicted to be even shorter than that of the United States. There is little doubt that over the next few years most of the world will be making a significant increase in the number of on-line purchases, both on a business-to-business and a business-to-consumer level. Second, there has never been a better time to raise money from financing sources such as venture capitalists. Flush with cash from already-successful Internet investments, venture capitalists are investing their newfound riches in businesses that have solid business models, unique technology solutions, and achievable profitability goals. While these conditions have created a highly competitive atmosphere, the fact remains that there has never been such an outstanding opportunity to harness the necessary resources to take a shot at making money in the millions.

No one could have anticipated the amount of wealth that would be generated from the creation of Internet companies. An entirely new industry has emerged in record-setting time, and it is only in its infant stage. Those entrepreneurs who keep pushing the capabilities of the Internet stand to be rewarded more than ever. The interviews in this book are meant to provide an inside look into the minds of some of the foremost Internet entrepreneurs today. May the insight these professionals provide serve to educate, motivate, and set the bar even higher for excellence and success in our wired world.

# 1

# The Great Minds of the Internet Revolution

## *An inside look at the new breed of Internet entrepreneurs*

The Internet has rewritten the rules of business. Never before have there been so many successful new companies established in such record-setting time, and an unprecedented percentage of those with the foresight and ambition to go for the gold have been rewarded handsomely for their efforts. Whereas it historically took companies decades for their stock to rise and build a solid market capitalization, Internet companies have been known to eclipse their brick-and-mortar brethren on their first day of trading. The Internet revolution makes anything possible. The only limitation is the extent to which creative minds can dream up new applications for the Internet.

Who builds and runs these Internet companies? Where and why do they thrive? And what about the culture that defines them? This chapter introduces the background on the industry that is fueling the new economic engine.

## Who Is the Internet Entrepreneur?

Internet entrepreneurs come from everywhere. There is no prescribed recipe for success. Anyone can make it, and potentially make it big, regardless of his or her previous experience, or lack thereof. You don't need to have a degree from Stanford or a Harvard MBA, only the hunger to succeed and the ambition and innovation to get you there—and, by some accounts, a constitution that needs very little sleep. Internet entrepreneurs are ex-CEOs and MBAs as well as college dropouts and techno geeks. Regardless of their background, all individuals who succeed work extremely hard and have unparalleled ambition and the courage to dream very big.

It is interesting to note the number of big-time executives leaving plush corporate lifestyles for a start-up opportunity—a move that almost always means cramped office space, a huge pay cut, grueling hours, and a lot of uncertainty. What motivates them to do it? Although it is different for each entrepreneur, there is an undeniable adrenaline rush to most start-ups. Some of these executives have already made big money; others are looking for their chance to lead; still others are just tired of the corporate grind. Most, however, are in search of the pot of gold at the end of the rainbow, pursuing a chance to cash in on an initial public offering (IPO) or sell their business at a profit. For those who succeed, there is nothing sweeter. However, it always takes a lot of hard work—

harder work usually than these individuals have ever encountered. Being part of an Internet company is an altogether different experience than the corporate track. Although most Internet companies do not survive and thrive, the experience of starting such a company is an unforgettable ride that frequently enhances an individual's skills in the end (probably because the entrepreneur has to do the jobs of at least four people).

Universities, too, are encouraging entrepreneurship, either by forming their own venture funds, as Columbia University has done, or holding entrepreneurial contests, which is the case at Massachusetts Institute of Technology (MIT). Venture capitalists have even made their way into college campuses to fund start-up ventures by individuals still enrolled in school. The fact of the matter is that great Internet entrepreneurs do not need to be tucked a way in a large corporation for twenty years to develop business skills. They need to be able to act decisively, alter a business model on a second's notice, and accurately forecast the future of their industry. Someone who is twenty-eight can just as easily meet these requirements as someone who is fifty-eight years of age. This does not mean that the older individual with more experience isn't a highly qualified candidate; it means only that individuals who in the past may not have been given a chance may be equally qualified to run their own businesses. For those with the right skills and experience and (not inconsequentially) the right personnel working with them, the door is now open for everyone to take a shot at becoming an Internet entrepreneur.

### Serial Entrepreneurs

Not content with having started one successful Internet business, often the great minds of the Internet revolution quickly move on to new ventures, thus spawning a new type of entrepreneur—the serial entrepreneur. Take, for instance, Sabeer Bhatia, the founder of Hotmail. Bhatia sold his business for hundreds of millions of dollars to Microsoft Corp., and one year later, he was back with another top-secret start-up, spending countless hours in cramped office space and eating leftover takeout. Another example is Jim Clark, founder of Netscape Communications and Silicon Graphics, who after making more money personally than most Fortune 500 companies in a matter of a few years, added two more feathers, Healtheon and Shutterfly.com, to his cap. Both men's stories attest to the fact that there is an undeniable magic about starting and growing an Internet company. They further prove that, for some people at least, the allure of the Internet start-up goes beyond just getting rich quick.

### Tomorrow's Leaders

Start-ups are really the new American dream. From the perspective of employment, some argue that the real prestige in business now lies with Internet and technology firms. There used to be a lot more prestige associated with working for a big-name firm that has been around for a long time and offers stability. People would work for the same company for thirty years and the company, it was thought, would take care of its people. Although this is still true to some extent, working for a start-up is now a very good thing. People dream about getting in on the ground floor of a start-up, with a fistful of options, going public within a couple of years, and then retiring early. This is impossible to do when going to work for an older public company. First, in the established public company, stock options are usually reserved for senior managers; second, the stock is unlikely to be as active as that of an Internet company's stock.

Because the Internet is so young, it remains to be seen what impact the number of younger professionals opting away from the larger companies will have on their bottom line in years to come. Will there be a whole new class of larger companies to emerge from the Internet era, fueled by younger and more ambitious individuals? Will the new venture capital model of fewer employees who are all partners outlive and outperform larger firms, such as PriceWaterhouseCoopers, Deloitte and Touche, and Andersen Consulting? Although there is no way to tell for sure, these firms may not have the abundance of talent in the future that they have today.

MBAs, for example, have always been an excellent bellwether for the current state of the economy. How much are they earning fresh out of graduate school? What are the hot industries? What types of positions are they being offered? Over the past three years, the answers to these questions are 180 degrees different from previous years. Especially at the top MBA programs, such as Stanford, Harvard, and Wharton, where the McKenzies, Morgan Stanleys, and Goldman Sachs of the world go for their fresh talent every year, fewer and fewer graduates are taking the corporate route. They are instead opting for positions in venture capital, an Internet company, or they are starting their own businesses altogether.

## SUCCESS AT LIGHT SPEED

The past five years have seen the creation of record-setting wealth for many people involved with a single indus-

try. Renowned Internet entrepreneurs like Steve Case of
AOL and Jerry Yang and David Filo of Yahoo! have
helped to produce hundreds of instant millionaires, from
every type of employee. Not only has it been incredibly
lucrative for their employees, but the general public has
been able to cash in as well. If you had invested $1,000 in
AOL at the beginning of 1998, it would have been worth
approximately $118,400 only two years later. Thus the
great minds of the Internet revolution are not only creating wealth for themselves, they are also creating it for
everyone around them and helping to fuel the economy as
a whole. And while it is true that for every success story
it is impossible to ignore the equal number of start-ups
that won't survive, both those that make it to the public
markets and those that are bought out are, on average,
cashing in for millions.

## THE LAND OF OPPORTUNITY

The number of new Internet companies that have
achieved a powerful position within our economy is unprecedented. One reason is that it is relatively easy to
start an Internet company. Get a URL (i.e., a Web address
and domain name) and a logo and print up business cards
and you "officially" have your own business. In addition,
the amount of venture capital pouring into new ventures
has been staggering. The most amazing part is that the
Internet industry is still in the early stages of development and there'll be a whole new wave of companies
within the next five to ten years.

What's next for Internet entrepreneurs? The Internet
is still extremely underused by the majority of the United

States and the world population. An incredible overseas explosion in use of the Internet is anticipated. The Internet is also still too expensive for many individuals. The costs associated with buying a computer and paying monthly charges will soon disappear or be drastically reduced as new programs bundle services together and as broadband access permeates the homes of Americans, who will be able to access the Internet through either their televisions or high-speed phone lines. For those individuals for whom the Internet is already an integral part of their lives, their reliance on online communication and commerce will only continue to grow in popularity as new services are introduced. For the would-be Internet entrepreneur, the key is to stay a couple of steps ahead of the Internet revolution and determine which products and services are going to be needed next.

## WHERE ARE THE DIGITAL CITIES OF TOMORROW?

Silicon Valley was first and remains the most renowned Internet community, but now there are Internet enclaves all across the United States. From Silicon Alley in New York City to the Netplex in Washington D.C. to Route 128 in Boston, Internet fever is spreading fast. What makes for an Internet community? Usually it starts out with a major Internet company establishing a presence in the area, followed by a number of smaller Internet companies setting up offices nearby. Sometimes it is the presence of a strong venture capital firm that is dedicated to making local investments in Internet and technology companies. Other times it is an incubator firm such as idealab! or eCompanies that hatches some very successful newcomers that are committed to staying in a given geographic location.

It is extremely important for Internet companies to be located near other companies that could become future partners or customers. Although the global nature of the Internet would make it seem that physical location would be irrelevant, the opposite is true. Because great importance is attached to strategic relationships with other companies, Internet start-ups are eager to be brought under the wings of a community in hopes they will break through with a couple of mutually beneficial deals. Venture capital firms, for example, are known for brokering deals between companies they have investments in and forming their own *keiretsu,* or network, of companies. Even city councils are getting involved. Recognizing the effect that a wave of Internet companies can have on a local economy, they are trying to create advantages for companies to set up shop in their cities. The number of valleys of Internet entrepreneurs across the world will only increase. As new areas become the digital cities of tomorrow, major population centers that do not attract such businesses soon will be in danger of losing economic steam.

## The Internet Culture

The management style of some Internet entrepreneurs has also generated a lot of attention. Internet entrepreneurs have used varying levels of creative management and work styles to attract and retain their employees, from allowing pets at work to providing all employees with BMW Z3s to accepting jeans as the work uniform of choice. In such a hot marketplace for individuals with technical and other Internet-related skills, it becomes increasingly important to make sure your employees are very happy at every level. This can mean anything—from throwing pizza parties once a month to having happy-hour meetings to discuss how to create a better work environment. Most Internet companies have their own unique environment, usually created by the employees who work there. The key is allowing these individuals to turn the workplace into the type of environment they want, instead of mandating a rigid office culture.

## Options, Options, Options

The new breed of Internet entrepreneurs wants options, and lots of them. From entry-level positions to entrepreneurs forming their own companies, stock options are the path to riches for everyone. Often, start-up Internet entrepreneurs even work solely for equity, forgoing a paycheck to put the money back into the company to hire additional employees or purchase necessary assets. In fact, individuals at every level are taking huge cuts in salary to get a larger number of stock options. The term *stock options* has taken on almost a magical ring in the last couple of years. It has also become the most powerful currency when trying to hire a key manager or member of the management team. Stock options, simply put, have become the most fantasized about and, in many cases, realistic path to wealth for hundreds of Internet entrepreneurs, employees, and investors.

## What About Profitability?

Profitability was once the primary bellwether of success for a company. Even in the Internet age, the move to profitability is beginning to be prized in commerce companies instead of the empty calories of top-line growth. For private companies, it is in most cases only a matter of time before they fold if they remain unprofitable. For public companies, if they are not profitable or moving toward profitability, it means declining stock prices and investor dissatisfaction. These fundamentals hold true even for Internet companies.

Although it undoubtedly takes time to grow any business, venture capitalists have generally felt that the opportunities presented by the Internet are so great they have been willing to bankroll an Internet company longer than usual to make sure they are able to position themselves properly in the marketplace. Many private Internet companies received millions of dollars in venture capital knowing they would not record profits for years into the future. Even a public Internet company such as Amazon.com, with a market capitalization of more than $20 billion, has yet to earn a nickel of profit. In fact, the majority of public Internet companies are unprofitable. The business model has instead been more focused on registered users, page views, and other intangibles believed to create value over the long term. This often has meant building the technology, attracting unique users, and inking the right strategic partnerships that will enable the business to go public or be sold. Because so many companies made it to the public markets without ever having been profitable, it became a much more "digestible" business model to forecast negative earnings for the foreseeable future. The owners, employees, and investors are all getting very rich—but the companies are not making any money. So who's losing?

The reality is that a business can only stand to lose

money for so long. In the end, it is investors who are left holding the bag if they hold shares of stock that plummet in value. Not surprisingly, the values on which Internet companies are built and measured are reversing themselves to a degree, now that Wall Street is refusing to look the other way on issues such as profitability.

The stock market has been a major impetus in the creation of new wealth for Internet entrepreneurs, and although Internet companies are coming under greater scrutiny after some failings, the public and investment community at large remain convinced that the Internet sector is just in its beginning and there is no time like the present to try and get in on the ground floor to reap rewards in the coming years. Will some of these stocks eventually fade away with little to no trading volume? Probably. Yet those that make it will become the Coca-Colas and Gillettes of tomorrow.

Though not actually an industry itself, the Internet has fundamentally changed almost every industry, opening the doors to a wave of entrepreneurship within our country. You can now do almost anything online, from buying a car to bidding to get plastic surgery. The number of new businesses being started is unprecedented and will only continue into the foreseeable future. If you do not think the Internet is going to affect your business or industry, you are wrong. As Andy Grove of Intel Corp. has noted, any business that does not have an Internet component will be gone in five years.

So sit back and learn from some leading Internet entrepreneurs. This book shares the secrets of nine Internet executives, each at various stages of development with their businesses, although all are still gunning to make their start-ups bigger and stronger.

# 2

# Startups.com

*With high-profile financial backers and partners, Startups.com is poised to capitalize on the wave of new ventures popping up across the country*

The story of Startups.com is a perfect example of how a consummate entrepreneur, who knows firsthand what it takes to run a start-up business, took the time to capitalize on a niche worth grabbing. As its name implies, Start ups.com's business is helping other start-ups succeed. Using its rich database of information about service providers in a wide variety of disciplines as an asset, Start ups.com helps new business owners select the right vendors and combination of services their businesses need to successfully get off the ground. The Web site takes business owners through an in-depth needs assessment by asking very specific questions—about their office

furniture, wiring, security, and accounting needs—then
Startups.com identifies the best service providers for
them.

The company is able to offer users of its site highly
favorable prenegotiated deals with qualified service providers that it contracts with, online planning tools and
resources, as well as the latest office automation techniques. In addition, each client is assigned a business
start-up specialist to be a personal consultant. In short,
Startups.com expects fast-track businesspeople to come
to the site and be able to do almost anything: order furniture, find office space, set up accounting and healthcare
services—all sorts of tasks that would normally require

## *Fast-Track Facts*

| | |
|---|---|
| ***Founder*** | Donna Jensen, launched the online service in early 2000 |
| ***Business model*** | Business-to-business information and services portal |
| ***Funding*** | Garage.com, Silicon Valley Bank, Venture Law Group, Vivid Studios |
| ***Business/Vendor Partners*** | BT Commercial and Grubb & Ellis (real estate); Lindsey Furr (office furniture); Exodus, Sun Microsystems, IBM Corp., Compaq, and Dell Computer (technology) |
| ***Clients/Customers*** | eVite, Google.com, EquipmentLeasing.com—any business that's moving fast and focused on its core business, revenues, and not getting off track |

dozens of phone calls, in-person meetings with vendors, and above all, time. In return, Startups.com charges clients a fee for its services and earns commissions on online purchases. It also accepts equity from qualified companies (frequently angel- or venture-backed client companies) in exchange for a percentage of its fees and earns additional revenue through sponsorships and some advertising on the site.

Donna Jensen, the CEO of Startups.com, tells her tale of success in the dot-com world. From her story we glean advice and insights to help other Internet business entrepreneurs.

## KNOWING YOUR STUFF

Jensen grew up in California's Central Valley and San Diego. She dropped out of college at age 19 to start her first company, Le Gourmet, a wholesale baking company that produced individually wrapped cookies and muffins that were sold at hundreds of 7-Elevens, delis, and cafes throughout southern California. Although the company was profitable, "I was young and I didn't know much about business, which led me to understand that I had a lot to learn," she says.

After three years of running Le Gourmet, Jensen went back to school to finish her undergraduate degree at San Diego State. After graduating, she worked for two years as an account representative for Airborne Express before deciding to go to business school. She chose Northwestern's Kellogg because of its reputation as a leading marketing school. After business school, she worked for several Dun & Bradstreet companies, including Nielsen Media Research in New York, D&B Software in Atlanta, D&B France in Paris, D&B Healthcare in Chicago, and IMS France.

Upon returning from France in 1996, she joined VentureOne in San Francisco, an information research firm that tracks venture financings for start-up companies. She worked there for two years (until the company's purchase by Reuters) as an executive in charge of product development and marketing. During her time at VentureOne, "living and breathing the start-up and VC world," she fell in love with the start-up industry. She read thousands of business plan briefs and got to know many of the key players.

But although she was involved in the start-up industry through her work at VentureOne, she felt as if she wasn't genuinely a part of it, but was just watching it happen. "I caught the start-up bug myself," she says, "and just wanted to get out there on my own. I knew I had it in me to run a company and the timing was right."

The reason Jensen picked a service niche for her business had a lot to do with her background and what she saw as an urgent need. As part of the business-to-business service industry at VentureOne, Jensen says she "got to know what defined a company's success and what was responsible for its failure." And, she says, "I really thought that I could provide a service that could help [businesses] free up their time, so they could be as successful as possible, and use the Internet in doing so."

She also always knew she wanted to start another company, it was just "a matter of the stars all lining up." After two years at VentureOne, she was ready to start a company, had some good industry connections, and suddenly got an idea that fit well with her skills.

Her original idea was inspired by Garage.com, a site that uses the capabilities of the Web to streamline the fund-raising process for start-ups. About a month after Garage.com launched, Jensen attended a VC event in Orange County where Guy Kawasaki, founder and CEO of Garage.com, and Mark Cuban, founder and CEO of Broadcast.com, were keynote speakers. "Both made incredibly captivating and inspirational speeches about starting and running successful start-ups. They spoke about moving fast, focusing on the core business and revenues, and not getting off track. I asked myself how I could help start-ups move faster and increase their chances for success and came up with the idea for a portal that aggregates advice from successful entrepreneurs: tips about time-saving tools and templates, benchmarks, prequalified service providers, and discounted products."

When she pitched the idea to entrepreneurs at the conference the next day, it received rave reviews because it addressed their greatest concerns about "not being able to hire the right people fast enough" and "not being able to move fast and focus on the right things." Probing deeper, Jensen learned that what keeps start-ups from focusing and moving as fast as they want to is the plethora of administrative issues that absorb their time. In the beginning stage of any company, these tasks tend to fall on the CEO's plate. For a CEO who might be a skilled engineer or businessperson by trade, these administrative issues can be overwhelming.

So Jensen decided to get in touch with Gargage.com's Kawasaki, and she e-mailed him her concept for a new company that would be a perfect partner for his company. A week later, she formally pitched the idea to him, and he was immediately supportive.

"Guy is a revolutionary," she says, "someone who's always willing to take risks and go for it. He's also a brilliant evangelist—the best ever."

## GETTING THE RIGHT PEOPLE ON BOARD

Before she could sell her idea, Jensen needed to come up with a name for her company. She went through the exercise of coming up with as many possibilities as she could, taking into consideration competitors, benefits, client characteristics, and the services her site would offer. Ultimately, she decided on the name that factually represented her clientele. Unfortunately, the Startups.com domain name was already owned by somebody in Nashua, New Hampshire. Jensen called him and spoke with him about her vision for Startups.com. As an entrepreneur himself, he wouldn't sell the name to her until he was convinced she meant to do something truly business transforming with it. In the end, he fully endorsed the concept and sold Jensen the Starups.com name for a mutually acceptable price.

Jensen's next step was to put together as many elements as she could before going out to look for capital. Based on what she'd seen happen with other companies, she knew a major success factor would be having the right partners right from the start. Attracting high-level people to your venture and getting their support and guidance is crucial, because it spurs a lot of other people to believe in your idea as well.

Garage.com made total sense as a primary partner. The day after Jensen pitched the idea to Kawasaki (which he loved), he pitched it to John Dean, the chairman of

Silicon Valley Bank, and Craig Johnson, the chairman of Venture Law Group. Both of them loved the idea, too. Their passion dovetailed with Jensen's: The tagline for Garage.com is, "We start up start-ups." Silicon Valley Bank is the major bank for start-ups in Silicon Valley, and Venture Law Group is one of the only law groups completely dedicated to serving start-up companies. They wanted to meet with Jensen.

Kawasaki, Johnson, and Dean ended up being Jensen's first board members, and Johnson agreed to represent the new venture, believing that Startups.com was going to fulfill a critical (and sometimes neglected) need among start-up companies.

To successfully launch a service-oriented Web site, Jensen needed to find someone with a strong background in outsourcing infrastructure services. Says Jensen, "I wanted someone who had rich experience in the outsource arena, who could help me understand this area better and how to approach it." Luckily, she discovered Intellisource, a Connecticut-based company that provides outsourced infrastructure support for Fortune 500 companies. She called the firm's CEO, Charles Gibbons, introduced herself, and told him what she was doing. "Essentially, Startups.com is a tiny Intellisource, except [it is] targeting start-up companies, and with a Web component, which Intellisource does not have," she explains. The CEO came out to the West Coast and met Startups. com's board members. "It took a couple of months of my convincing him," says Jensen, "but [Gibbons] finally decided that this was certainly worth his time." Gibbons became a Startup.com board member.

A crucial part of starting an Internet company is using your contacts. This is especially important before a site launches, in order to create buzz. Jensen did this through every avenue she could: partners, board members, investors, service providers, and clients. The company also throws parties at a place called The Loop, a venue for regular meetings which bring together a hand-picked group of CEOs from top start-up companies.

Startups.com closed its financing in July 1999 and launched in February 2000. It already had clients before it launched—even though it wasn't actively seeking them! These clients simply heard about Startups.com and came to the company for help. "You expect it to be a real challenge to drum up business and bring in revenues, and we're probably one of the few Internet companies that, prior to launch, was bringing in revenues," marvels Jensen.

### Startups.com's Key Success Factors

- Service teams of business start-up specialists in areas such as facilities, IT, HR, payroll, and finance
- Database of leading service providers in each specialty area
- Strategic investor and vendor partnerships

## GETTING THE MOST FROM YOUR BOARD

Jensen advises most entrepreneurs to put together a board even before going out to look for funding. An advisory board gives credibility to the enterprise and helps you to attack your own ideas beforehand (before the investors do) and fine-tune them as much as possible. Jensen, her board of directors, and her advisory board spent several months working on their business plan, testing it, and getting it to a point where they felt extremely comfortable with it, before they sought funding.

"The ability to listen to people, to incorporate their ideas, to know that you don't have all the answers is critical," says Jensen. "There are people out there who have had a variety of experiences, and some of those experiences can be leveraged to help you fine-tune your business model."

Of all of her advisers, Jensen says that Craig Johnson single-handedly had the greatest impact on her business model because he championed the service component. Originally, Jensen's idea was to pool information resources for start-up companies and provide a way to help clients find the right service provider. Johnson challenged the notion that having a portal with top-flight advice was good enough. He advocated that adding a service component for providing direct, hands-on help to business users would make Startups.com a much stronger proposition.

As a board adviser, Johnson prompted thinking about revenue streams and the profitability side of things and made Jensen rethink a whole different business model—one that's based on sustainability and building a business that could survive with or without the Internet. Thus, Startups.com would not only bring ideas together, it would also use the Web to actually streamline infrastructure services for fledgling companies. "Having a model that is both analog and digital buffers the volatility [in the Internet space]," says Jensen. Johnson's challenges were difficult, Jensen admits, but he forced her to look at her business plan in terms of building a company "that would last for the duration, not a quick-hit, go-public."

The rest of her board is equally seasoned, too, which is an asset considering the young age of most of the employees at Startups.com. (At thirty-five, Jensen is the oldest employee.) "The board balances out our exuberance and determination with real experience," says Jensen. Other board members include John Kohler, a venture capitalist who only invests in dot-com businesses and is a founding partner at Ledley Venture Management; Steve Bacher, the lead attorney for start-ups at Wilson, Sansini; and Amanda Duckworth, a founding partner at Tom Weisel Partners. (Tom Weisel was the founder of Montgomery Securities, which for many years was the top investment bank for taking venture-backed start-ups public.) Finally, there is Jack Pess, the CEO of Business Resource Group, a large furniture and space planning company. Pess has twenty-five years of experience in the business-to-business professional services industry.

Jensen also believes that strategic partners are the key to success for Internet companies. "Things are moving so fast, you cannot build an empire on your own in a year or in eighteen to thirty-six months." Instead, the only way to succeed is to find good strategic partners and leverage their technology, markets, clientele, and their promotions to help you move as fast as you can.

Jensen pursued contacts she knew through Venture-One, who then introduced her to potential candidates as board members and advisers. Thus Jensen identified prospects likely to be open to her ideas, but she still had to meet with them to convince them that she was the right person to implement the idea. "[Investors are] not going to [attach] their name to a company or a person—and the person is always the most important thing in the eye of investors—that they don't think can [see the idea through]."

Jensen presented herself as a kindred spirit to her new partners, as "someone who is entrepreneurial and willing to take risks and put everything into [making her idea succeed]." They also knew she loved the start-up industry. "This has been a passion of mine ever since I started my professional career, and especially since I was at VentureOne, I've lived and breathed start-ups," she says.

To guide the company toward becoming a provider of hands-on services, Jensen needed to find a partner that had experience in this area. She found a partner by posting an advertisement in an online job board for the Bay area called Craig's List. Justin Segal had previously started two companies, a real estate accounting-software company and a property management company that he founded with his brother in Texas. "Justin had the appropriate experience and is a true entrepreneur," she says. "I can't imagine a better partner."

The bottom line: The first thing Jensen did to make her company a success was to get leaders in the start-up industry to buy into her concept. Then she was able to get their advice while creating her business model.

### Advice to Other Internet Entrepreneurs

Find great board members and advisers who ask the tough questions up-front and challenge your model, making you prove you can make money off it.

Monitor what human resources you need to take your company to the next level—and always hire *before* you think you need people.

## FINDING FINANCING

Getting money for Startups.com was a simple, efficient process. Jensen believes this is because she chose to go through Garage.com instead of looking directly for angel investors (i.e., wealthy individuals who invest directly in start-ups) on her own. Garage is selective; it has received thousands of business plans but has taken on only twenty-five to thirty companies since it started. It does such a good job weeding through business plans that investors trust its choices. People in the industry know that Garage.com's method for helping companies secure financing (and for helping investors find companies) works. Having witnessed many companies raise capital through Venture-One, Jensen felt as if she knew the process and could have gone directly to venture capitalists. But she recognized that Garage.com provides a great vehicle for attracting capital quickly.

> *The great entrepreneurs are not the ones that think about exiting their business right away.*

In addition, when Jensen went out to get financing, the benefits of the feedback from her advisers became clear, because she was able to open and close her first round in five weeks.

This kind of speed in getting financing is highly un-usual. Even Jensen admits that it's something that doesn't happen often. Her recommendation? "To the ex-tent that you can, get out there, test [your idea] on the market, get advisers who are truly credible, and try to get to know people that you don't know." And "stretch yourself when you network," she says. "Not just your friends, but people that you don't know and are the most well respected in your industry. That just goes miles."

Jensen notes, "You read all these articles about there being so much money out there, and there is more money in the venture capital coffers than at any time in the his-tory of venture capital. Adding to that is all the money available from angel investors. Companies such as Micro-soft and Netscape and Oracle have created lots of mil-lionaires who now are interested in investing in their entrepreneurial brethren. What we are finding is a huge number of angel investors who are eager to invest in good ventures."

She decided to select the investors who were the best strategic fit—those that had one or more key characteris-tics, infrastructure expertise, or connections in an impor-tant geographic area (e.g., Boston, Seattle, L.A., New York, and Austin) and were active investors. In the end, she selected twenty-one angel investors. In addition, she met with a number of venture capital firms and ulti-mately selected Redleaf Venture Management. Redleaf is a young firm that had just raised its second fund and is totally dedicated to dot-com companies. Its philosophy is to add value by helping start-ups set up their infra-structure—a perfect fit for what Startups.com was doing.

"Startups.com was very fortunate. We went from opening the round [of funding] on June 18, 1999, to closing in five weeks flat," says Jensen. "My advice to other entrepreneurs is to put the right pieces of the puzzle together from the beginning. Don't spend too much time creating a hundred-page business plan because nobody's going to read it. Investors prefer a ten- to twenty-page business plan, and probably as a starting point, a simple PowerPoint presentation that gets across who you are, what market you're trying to serve, its size and potential, what your product is, and how it's differentiated from all of the others out there."

## FINDING GOOD TALENT

Jensen believes that one of the most important tasks for an Internet start-up is finding good talent. "People are always what it comes down to," she says. "You've got to be the right person to execute and to lead, and you've got to have the right team members in place who complement you and help you get to where you want to be."

Unfortunately, finding those team members can be extremely difficult. "There are so many things that you want to think about when you're hiring people to make sure you're building the kind of culture and company that you want," says Jensen. "Obviously, I want to hire the brightest people that I can find. I want those people to be entrepreneurial in spirit and comfortable in a pretty unstructured, casual environment. I want people who don't need a job description that they're going to hold you to in six months. My greatest challenge, and the challenge for most entrepreneurs, is finding the right people fast enough."

There is virtually no unemployment in the professional job sector in Silicon Valley right now; it's one of the easiest places in the world for qualified people to get a job. Jensen received approximately 1,000 résumés, and interviewed more than 100 people while looking for her core management team. In retrospect, she says that the online resources for finding people are the best resources out there. "It's demonstrative of the way the world is going in the service area," she says. "The Web is not just for entertainment; it's not just for e-commerce. It's a way of conducting business."

She ended up finding two of her employees through Craig's List (www.listfoundation.org), an online job board, and got three others from Garage.com's job bank. A friend recommended another employee. While using a headhunter can be good (especially if you're looking for a president or other high-level people), there's no substitute for scanning through résumés yourself and getting a sense of a person through a phone conversation. Jensen says the headhunter she's been working with has, almost without fail, sent her candidates who are qualified but not a good fit for her organization. "They can't screen for that as well as I can in a quick phone conversation," she explains.

She also recommends that start-ups monitor what human resources they need to take their company to the next level (and that you always hire before you think you need people, because it always takes longer to find people than you think)."The companies that are going to win on the Internet are companies that hire faster, because it's the people that allow you to move as fast as you need to move."

## CREATING A CASUAL SPIRIT

Another important aspect of developing a company is creating a good work environment, and Jensen had already determined the kind of corporate culture she wanted to promote when she started her business. She wanted an environment that was casual and spirited. (She brings her dog to work.) She's also tried to develop an environment where everybody feels a sense of ownership. Everyone at Startups.com has options in the company, and everyone is involved in establishing company policy. Team members talk frequently about the company's core values, its mission, its culture, and how to preserve that culture, especially as the company grows.

### Bottom Line: Is Startups.com Profitable Yet?

Startups.com is making money and plans to be cash-flow-positive sometime in the middle of 2001. Dollars will go into supporting expansion and development. The company wants to set up offices in different cities: Boston, Austin, Seattle, and Los Angeles. It also plans to promote its business and offer franchise opportunities abroad.
"We're in this for the long run," says Jensen. "We're building a company that offers the promise of large revenue and profit potential on the Web, but regardless of what happens with the Web, we'll still have a revenue stream to support the company."

Jensen believes that a company called Startups.com has to be entrepreneurial. The company's mission is to serve entrepreneurs, and because it's a part of the start-up community, employees need to be entrepreneurial in nature. Jensen has instituted monthly margarita parties and a unique vacation policy: three weeks paid time off plus five ski days. Because her employees often work nights and weekends, that's her way of saying thank-you and of encouraging them to keep balance in their lives.

> ## Most Unique Management Practice
>
> Startups.com's vacation policy: three weeks paid time off, plus five ski days.

## Cultivating Partners

Startups.com determines what needs to be done and then brings in strategic partners, which have been prescreened and have excellent references, to support its business-to-business service model. Companies it is working with right now include real estate companies such as BT Commercial and Grubb & Ellis; furniture companies such as BRG, OP Contracts, and Lindsey Furr; and technology companies such as Exodus, Sun Microsystems, IBM Corp., Compaq, and Dell Computer.

"These companies, because they are so large, are set up to service large corporations. That's the low-hanging fruit for them," explains Jensen. "But it's difficult for them to identify and sell to start-ups. On the other hand, they all recognize that start-ups—Internet start-ups in particular—are driving the economy into the future, and they want to get to them as early as possible." Many of Jensen's vendor-partners have a budget specifically di-

rected toward targeting start-up companies and see
Startups.com as a way to access that market segment. All
of the aforementioned companies approached Startups.
com (not the other way around) because they see the
value of its business model and how it can help them.
"We're a channel for them; we've got the name here in the
Valley," says Jensen.

IBM, for example, found Startups.com through
Garage.com's network of investors, of which IBM is a
part, and initiated a discussion about the possibilities of
a strategic partnership. Many of Startups.com's other
technology partners were referred to the company by Exodus, the large Web hosting company. "If you can attract
a few people in an area such as technology, where everyone knows everybody, you'll inevitably get some people
who believe in and are excited about what you're doing.
Then it has the snowball effect. You get all these calls.
That's what happened: I just got tons of calls."

In other cases, how does Jensen know whom to contact within other big companies she views as potential
strategic partners? Frequently you know someone who
knows someone else and through him or her you can connect with the right person. "And if not, you just make a
phone call and find out who the key person is, and you
can get that information through a directory."

Other partners selling their products and services
through Startups.com include Vivid Studios, a presti-
gious Web design firm in the San Francisco area, and Ice
Wireless, a small networking company that takes customers through a needs-assessment online to help them
choose cell phones. "They'll order it for you, set it up for
you, transfer your service from one phone to another, and

deliver it to you," says Jensen of their turnkey concept. Finally, there's Simpata, a benefits administrator.

## PLANNING FOR DOWN THE ROAD

Jensen has mapped out a three-year plan for Startups. com. It takes the company from offering business start-up services to a whole new range of services where business users can leverage their expertise in new ways.

"You won't just meet with a real estate person and go through catalogs to buy furniture and fill out physical paperwork for your healthcare or payroll [departments]," says Jensen. "Absolutely everything will be done online. That's the direction that I'm taking this company. You fill out one profile, one credit application, and [that information is] populated into [automated] forms for all the different vendors, so you [as the business entrepreneur] don't have to keep filling out paperwork. It saves you a lot of time. We preselect those services and products that are the best and most cost-effective and that match with the benchmarks of the industry. You'll always have the ability to customize and order the bells and whistles, but we will merchandise specifically those products and services that are the benchmarks. These are the five desk configurations most start-ups choose; here're a dozen chairs and the benefits of each, for example.

"This is the future of business infrastructure and how business is going to be run. The Web gives you a billion options, but the companies that are going to help businesses run more efficiently are companies like Start ups.com that preevaluate solutions, narrow the choices, make the information simple, and make the decision-making process simple and fast. It still takes too long to sift through all the information on the Web to figure out what cell phone to purchase, what chair is the right chair, what healthcare benefit administrator you should choose. We'll do all that work and bring it all together in one place to make it simple."

### Vision of the New Service Economy

"The days of the entrepreneur who does everything himself and feels that . . . only his ideas are the right ideas is past. That's a recipe for failure in today's economy, because you can't know everything, your ideas aren't always the best ideas, and you're not always the best person for every part of your business."

Traditionally, service companies are not scalable in that each one requires a different solution, Jensen explains. What the Web can do is reduce the amount of face-time required to deliver a service by putting information, resources, and project-management tools online. Startups. com puts the original qualifications form, the in-depth needs-assessment forms, project-management tools, business calendars, and alerts and order forms online, where clients can see everything and anything at any time. The ability to read instructions and tutorials and to download templates are things that would normally require someone to talk to you on the phone, fax you something, e-mail you something, come to see you in person, or give you a presentation. Now all those services can be accessed on the Web—"although you always want to have a person behind it," Jensen advises, "because that's what produces client confidence in your service."

Like her fellow Internet revolutionaries, Jensen doesn't think the Internet is a fad. She believes it is just another communication vehicle—one that brings all the other vehicles together worldwide. "It makes communication faster and more far-reaching than anything we've ever seen before," she says. "It's a total fallacy to think of the Web as a community, that the dot-com companies are web businesses. Amazon.com is not a web company; it's a bookseller. Startups.com is not a web business. We are a service company that leverages the Web to significantly streamline the way businesses are set up."

Jensen has already started to market Startups.com abroad. She's met with top venture capitalists in Israel and has gotten the business moving in that direction already. One of her clients, Tradeum, is a hot Israeli company backed by Israel Seed Capital, that is setting up an office in the United States. "Most venture-backed companies in Israel do come to the United States, typically Silicon Valley or Boston," she says.

That too will change, she believes. The same thing that's happened here with Internet companies is beginning to happen in Europe and in Asia as well. They're just in the infancy stages in terms of venture capital and the start-up industry. So not only will Startups.com market its services abroad, it plans to partner with companies abroad—and potentially provide franchise opportunities to qualified individuals who can help it reach the rest of the world.

And that, says Jensen, is the most exciting part: being able to come up with an idea and grow it from the very beginning into a service, a company, a product, or a web site that people can touch and feel and that affects their life in a positive way.

She likes the idea of helping companies set up a foundation that will support their growth going forward. "Being able to come in contact with these wonderful entrepreneurs, who have put so much of their brilliance and passion into their ventures, and being able to help them set up their company and take some things off their plate that could potentially keep them from being as successful as they hope to be—that is extremely rewarding," she says. Bringing together her own team members and giving them the opportunity to be a part of a start-up, seeing the excitement they feel, and watching them grow professionally and personally has been gratifying as well.

Jensen projects that the Internet companies that will be most successful are the ones using the Web to its full extent. By that, she means that the Web is not just a transaction vehicle, a communications vehicle, or a promotion vehicle. "Its different from any prior resource that we've used in business in that it encompasses all of these things," she says. "You can promote, you can communicate, and you can transact business." The companies that are doing it right are the ones bringing all of these elements together to create a client experience that makes buying online as natural as possible. "Doing that correctly is bringing them to the site and giving them rich content as well as a way to interact and ask questions and making the buying process as simple and intuitive as possible. In some way, the buying process should be a guided learning experience rather than just a catalog online that gives you a billion different things. The sites that are doing it right are leveraging all the powers of the Web to the full extent."

# 3

# VarsityBooks.com

## *The incredible ride to an IPO for the leading online retailer of college textbooks*

VarsityBooks.com sells new college textbooks online and has established a platform for marketing a variety of goods and services (in addition to textbooks) to the nation's fifteen million college students. VarsityBooks.com has sold textbooks to students in each of the fifty states at over 2,400 colleges and universities. According to Media Metrix, an audience ratings and e-commerce measurement service, www.varsitybooks.com has on numerous monthly occasions been the most visited college-oriented Web site.

Using the Internet, VarsityBooks.com is able to offer customers a convenient purchasing process and reduced prices. Its carefully selected and trained network of more than 1,000 student representatives promotes its products and brand on college campuses nationwide, so Varsity Books.com can, in effect, customize its marketing to the particular dynamics of each campus and reach students on a peer-to-peer basis.

VarsityBooks.com launched its Web site in August 1998 with the booklists for five schools. By the fall 1999 semester, it had increased the posted booklists to more than 300 colleges and universities. In addition, it launched partnership programs with thirteen different partner institutions.

To date, the company has raised $41.4 million in private funding. The first round, totaling $1.4 million, was led by angel investors and closed in July 1998. The second round, led by top East and West Coast venture capital firms FBR (Friedman, Billings, Ramsey) Technology Venture Partners and Mayfield Fund, totaled $10.0 million and closed in February 1999. The third round, led by Internet venture capitalists Tribune Ventures and Carlyle Venture Partners, totaled $30.0 million and closed in August and September 1999. The company filed its Registration Statement on Form S-1 with the Securities and Exchange Commission on October 15, 1999 and went public in early 2000.

## HEALING PAIN IN THE CONSUMER MARKET

VarsityBooks.com founder Eric J. Kuhn didn't necessarily set out to start his own Internet business. His training

### *Fast-Track Facts*

| | |
|---|---|
| **Founder** | Eric J. Kuhn, launched site in August 1998 |
| **Business Model** | Online retailer |
| **Funding** | FBR Technology Venture Partners, Mayfield Fund, Tribune Ventures, and Carlyle Venture Partners |
| **Business Partners** | Baker & Taylor book distributors, Citizens Scholarship Fund of America (CSFA) |

and education prepared him for a law career, and in December 1997, when he got the idea for VarsityBooks.com, he was practicing law in a large corporate firm in Miami. The idea actually came to him while he was in the firm's library. He remembered having read somewhere that the most successful businesses are those that heal some kind of "pain" that exists somewhere out there in the market. On that day in the library, he was remembering how frustrating and painful the experience of buying textbooks had been, both as an undergraduate and as a law student:

"The bookstores where I was virtually obligated to spend my money seemed to me to have benefited from some degree of immunity from free market dynamics," he says. "I know I did not pay a fair price for these texts. I wasted lots of time in line. And after spending all that time and money, I had to haul all these texts home with me. I felt, as a consumer, that I had been given very little choice."

The more he thought about this experience, the more he saw a clear and compelling opportunity for a Web-based service for college students—the largest single group of active Web users out there. Textbooks are an obligatory purchase for them all. In many cases, they resent the prices college bookstores charge and have little loyalty for what many consider to be a campus monopoly. Kuhn got more and more excited about this idea and became intrigued by the potential for the Web to transform this slice of everyday life.

VarsityBooks.com studied the college marketplace carefully—and liked what it found. According to Student Monitor LLP, a market research firm that focuses on college students and lifestyles, 95 percent of all college students use the Internet, spending an average of 5.6 hours per week online, with many of them using it for decision making about purchases. Furthermore, internal data from VarsityBooks.com indicates that 77 percent of its purchasers use the Internet at least once a day. Kuhn also buoyed his own findings with facts from other market researchers in determining his idea's market potential:

- College textbooks represent an estimated $3 billion to $5 billion market annually (Jupiter Communications).
- College students buy at three times the rate of adults on the Internet (Jupiter).
- More than 90 percent of all college students are online regularly, and most of them have at least one credit card. American college students in general represent an online market valued at more than $875 million a year (Jupiter).
- After tuition, college textbooks are the most expensive cost associated with a college education. Students spend approximately $300 (and up to $400) per semester on course books. In addition, textbook sales are the least profitable part of running a college store (National Association of College Stores).
- Most important, buying textbooks online saves students an average of between $9 and $24 per class (Atlantis Technology).

Calling upon a good law school friend of his, Tim Levy, who was then practicing in Washington, Kuhn talked the idea through with him, and within a week the two had incorporated VarsityBooks.com and developed a preliminary plan. They estimated that by eliminating costly overhead associated with the traditional brick-

and-mortar bookstore model, they could provide students major discounts on their textbooks.

Things happened quickly after that. Kuhn quit his law firm and moved to Washington D.C. In April 1998, he and Levy signed a strategic alliance with one of the country's leading book distributors, North Carolinabased Baker & Taylor, which enabled VarsityBooks.com to offer students access to approximately 2.5 million textbooks and trade books from more than 25,000 publishers. And in just a few months, they raised $1.4 million in seed financing.

When the site went live in August 1998, the primary focus was to deliver unbeatable customer service and a better textbook alternative for college students. The site featured comprehensive booklists for five of Washington D.C.'s largest universities, as well as a powerful mega-search engine that allowed students to quickly find their books by specific courses, professors, titles, authors, keywords, and ISBN numbers. The company did grassroots promotion for the site at the five largest D.C. area schools—Georgetown, George Mason, George Washington University, University of Maryland, and University of Virginia—and got an immediate positive reception.

"When I talked to students, I could see the lights go on instantly," says Kuhn. "[Many of them] e-mailed their friends at other campuses, and that first semester we sold books to thousands of students at schools in all fifty states. A new student revolution was born!"

Since that time, the company has experienced rapid growth on a number of levels: number of employees and student representatives, volume of sales, ability to offer customized course booklists, and financing. During the spring 1999 selling season, VarsityBooks.com sold textbooks to tens of thousands of students at most colleges and universities across the country. At that time, it posted the booklists for seventy-five schools and had a student campus representative network of over 300 students on campuses around the country.

VarsityBooks.com has created many unique aspects in its business model to make it decidedly different from all other competitors. In August 1999, it extended its selection and services to graduate students in law, medicine, and business. VarsityBooks.com also launched a unique partnership program that lets educational institutions nationwide outsource their entire new textbook operations. Partnership schools (e.g., colleges, universities, private high schools, and distance-learning programs) earn a portion of sales revenue (based on the breadth and depth of their partnership with VarsityBooks.com). They are also able to offer greater textbook purchasing convenience and discounts for students; create customized booklists for students online; and offer personalized student accounts and flexible payment options. Charter partners include Alaska Pacific University and the College of Aeronautics (Flushing, New York).

The company also offers its academic affiliates the option of endowing their own departmental scholarships with the funds shared by VarsityBooks.com. Through a partnership with Citizens Scholarship Fund of America (CSFA)—the country's leading educational nonprofit organization—professors, academic departments, or schools whose students buy from VarsityBooks.com can direct a share of those sales to CSFA's Dollars for Scholars program. This program is a network of more than 800 grassroots scholarships foundations in thirty-eight states and the District of Columbia that raise funds and provide financial and academic support to local students.

On the other side, students receive all of the benefits of the VarsityBooks.com service model: access from any location, at any hour, to customized class booklists and millions of book titles; a thirty-day return policy; and savings of up to 40 percent on new textbooks. (The company guarantees receipt of order within one to three business days at a flat shipping and handling rate of $4.95, regardless of order size). An optional registration process on the VarsityBooks.com site allows students to store all billing, shipping, and order history information in one secure location. Registered students benefit from greater personalized service every time they log on and faster ordering and sales checkout—taking the "pain" out of the book-buying experience.

One unique thing the company began offering in the fall of 1999 is an online "scratch" game and sweepstakes. Players use their mouse to scratch game cards and uncover prizes (e.g., CDs, a semester of free books, and portable MP3 players). If three of the same prizes are uncovered, the player wins that prize. Every time a person plays, she is entered into a drawing for a "digital dorm room," which includes a home theater sound system, a DVD player, digital camera, and other equipment.

Prognosis: VarsityBooks.com is considered the category leader according to most mainstream media covering this market segment, and Media Metrix has consistently rated VarsityBooks.com as one of the most-trafficked college-oriented sites during the peak back-to-school season. In the fall of 1999, the company launched a site redesign with the booklists for over 300 schools and had over 1,000 campus representatives working as marketers on their respective campuses. "And the leaders take the arrows," says Kuhn.

### VarsityBooks.com's Key Success Factors

○ Staffing that mixes energy and experience
○ Building an offline, on-the-ground network of student representatives who drive traffic to the site and who know better than anyone how to market on campus
○ Building a brand that's backed by value and a flawlessly executed service model
○ Using one-to-one marketing techniques
○ Maintaining focus on a primary goal despite other tangential opportunities and potential distractions

## ADDING A PERSONAL TOUCH

Kuhn says that some of the best advice he ever got was from his father, who told him "to connect with smart people and empower them with decision-making authority." A business is a group effort, and many people forget that. You can have the best idea in the world, but you can't make it happen if you are all by yourself. And other people won't be get excited about your idea unless you manage to create a working environment where people know that their ideas matter, that they can challenge your ideas and perceptions, and that they will be taken seriously by other members of the team.

Consequently, Kuhn says he's been in "recruiting mode" since day one. Everywhere he goes, as he meets people, he tries to find out what they're doing, where they are in their careers, what their strengths are, and whether they would be the proverbial "good fit" for VarsityBooks. com. He's starting to realize that this will be a continual part of his experience as he continues to build the company. "That's a constant part of everyone's job here, as far as I'm concerned," he says.

It is incredibly important to have the right mix of people to run a business in this industry. "As young as the dot-com space is," Kuhn says, "it's already littered with wreckage: businesses that may have had a compelling or sexy idea but didn't have the experience or the focus to follow through on initial promises." His staffing model to get around that syndrome mixes energy and experience. VarsityBooks.com has brought on board a number of seasoned individuals with years of experience in the book-selling industry, consumer marketing, customer service, and corporate IT. Coupling all of that collective expertise with younger people, who bring a "campus" perspective to the mix, the company has created a work environment where everyone is learning from each other continuously—with the overall goal, of course, of improving the customer experience. How does VarsityBooks.com create incentives for its employees? The sheer power of equity in the new economy is crucial to keeping people motivated and productive. Thus it has extended stock options both to its employees and to its lead student representatives on campuses around the country. The company has also instituted additional programs to help employees feel vested. These include traditional measures, such as competitive salaries and generous benefits, as well as significant professional growth and development opportunities to keep people interested and challenged. All employees are invited to give their opinions on all aspects of the business.

The company tries to maintain a positive work atmosphere that rewards accomplishments, encourages intelligent risks, and breeds creativity. Its office is open and casual. People ride their bikes to work and park them outside their cubicles. Suits and ties are worn by visiting vendors only. There is also a strong team element: Everyone applauds the accomplishment when someone secures a new booklist school or starts a representative program on a new campus. Kuhn and Levy don't necessarily spend a lot of time engineering the atmosphere; it's a bit artificial when people try that, and they think it would ring false. But the company does plan after-hours events frequently to give people a chance to bond and celebrate outside of the day-to-day business environment.

"Over and above all that," Kuhn says, "if you walked through the offices and cubicles and asked people what makes them get out of bed every morning, they'd tell you in some way that they feel they are part of a movement that is making students' lives better. We were first to offer students a way to save time and money by using the Web to buy their books. [We have a] sense . . . that Varsity-Books.com is an important part of what's happening in our culture and economy right now."

Another important aspect of VarsityBooks.com's approach to personnel is its network of student representatives. As enrolled students at their respective schools, the representatives provide feedback on their peers' needs and lifestyles, which allows VarsityBooks.com to customize its marketing approach to the particular dynamics of each campus. Student representatives reach potential customers wherever students gather—classrooms, student organizations, dormitories, and fraternities and sororities. VarsityBooks.com believes that its student representative network, combined with its campaigns, differentiates it and more effectively builds brand awareness, driving more traffic to its Web site than a traditional national or regional marketing campaign would.

## Approach to Personnel Management

After the customer, the second most important person is the skilled employee. "Without that person, offering value and service are impossible," says Kuhn. In addition to stock options extended to both its employees and its lead student representatives on campuses around the country, VarsityBooks.com includes traditional measures such as competitive salaries and generous benefits, as well as significant professional growth and development opportunities to keep people interested and challenged.

Because they are "the human face" of VarsityBooks.com, student representatives are chosen carefully. They undergo a thorough application and interview process and receive formal training on how to market on their campuses. They attend twice-yearly company retreats where they participate in marketing workshops and seminars, and have regular conference calls with their Varsity Books.com representative coordinators. Student representatives are active members of the VarsityBooks.com team. They've designed incredibly creative and effective programs on their campuses—everything from chalking

sidewalks and handing out flyers to launching Varsity
Books.com beach balls at sporting events and decorating
cars with VarsityBooks.com stickers. "No one knows better how to market on campus than the students themselves," says Kuhn. "That's the idea behind the entire rep
network."

## SPREADING THE WORD

VarsityBooks.com has begun to create a brand online—
"but not with patronizing, gross-out images in our
marketing materials," says Kuhn. Instead, brand development for this company is through "something deeper.
That's the trust and reputation for reliability we've
earned on campuses across the country."

Brand is an interesting concept. Millions of dollars
are spent by dot-coms on the advertising front, so it's
clear that brand is top-of-mind to a lot of people in the
Internet space. But VarsityBooks.com thinks people
sometimes get entranced by the "creative" that their
agencies bring in and forget the essential truth to branding—that it must be manifest in every single point of contact with your customer.

"Brand is the idea of your company that exists in
your customer's mind," explains Kuhn. "That brand gets
built over time by a series of small touches. How you answer your phones says something about your brand. Your
pricing communicates a great deal about the value of
your brand. Speed of delivery of your product and the
quality of the packaging says something about your
brand, too, and can buttress or detract from a positive
brand image in your customer's mind. What we are doing

is building a brand in everything we do. This isn't a short-term proposition. You can't wake up one day and pull a brand out of your ear."

That's not to say that VarsityBooks.com is minimizing the importance of seductive advertising and image, but its executives are aware that if that image isn't backed by value and a flawlessly executed service model, it's all for naught. Everything VarsityBooks.com does is based on the premise that students are aggressive and savvy consumers who want choice and recognize value when they see it. They can do the math. It's not a matter of installing a brand image in their brains. They are too smart for that. It's about giving them power and informed choice, and continually refining the service model to meet their needs better than anyone else.

VarsityBooks.com's network of student representatives is an enormous advantage in this area. The representatives are the company's eyes and ears on campus. They function as a sort of seismograph for campus trends and developments. The company is continuously refining its service model and business plans based on feedback it gets from this network. This vital communication loop allows the company to know students better than competitors and to tailor its messaging and service mix accordingly.

The company works hard to know students at a peer-to-peer level, and traffic to the site bears that out. "It would be easy to say that we will just keep doing what we've been doing all along, and we'll continue on as the leading online college bookseller," says Kuhn. "But it's not going to work that way. We'll always stick to our core business of selling books to students in a more affordable and convenient manner, but we will also do so much more," says Kuhn.

In everything VarsityBooks.com does, it focuses on the needs and desires of college students. The company plans on expanding its product and service mix based on what it learns about college students through its interaction with customers and its sales representative network every day. "I'm not saying that we are going to offer students every conceivable product they could possibly order online, but based on the knowledge and experience we've gained, we will be expanding our product mix strategically in the months ahead," explains Kuhn.

All companies like to make the claim that they "own" their category of business, but VarsityBooks.com has the bragging rights in the college space, if anyone does. It was the first to market and inspired several imitators. It has built an offline, on-the-ground force of student representatives to drive traffic to its site. It is partnering with prep schools, colleges, and distance-learning organizations in a way that lets them close down their campus stores and outsource their entire on-campus e-tail organization to a Web provider. And its traffic data, as recorded by Media Metrix, more than anything else, points up its relative dominance.

VarsityBooks.com is enough of a threat to other college textbook sellers that the immense trade organization in this market, the National Association of College Stores (NACS), is marshalling its legal resources to sue Varsity Books.com for making "false and misleading advertising claims." NACS is seeking injunctive relief against VarsityBooks.com and is challenging its claim to offer discounts of up to 40 percent. Although VarsityBooks.com believes this suit to be completely without merit, it also views it as significant vindication of the company's original idea. Most likely because of its leadership status, VarsityBooks.com was the only one of several potential online vendors to be singled out in this suit.

## FOCUSING CREATIVITY

Kuhn and his colleagues have learned a lot during their short time in business. Lesson one? The Internet industry never sleeps.

"When your model is Web-based, it's so much easier to modify your service mix and value proposition," says Kuhn. "We could do this, couldn't we?" is a constant mantra.

"Leadership requires continuously coming up with creative approaches to your target market, but also as important [is] maintaining focus on your goal despite other tangential opportunities and potential distractions. I would say balancing creativity with the need to focus is the biggest management challenge facing anyone in this industry."

Kuhn and his colleagues believe that there are several ways to attack that challenge. First and foremost, you must be extremely tough on your value proposition. Does your idea cure some "pain" that is out there in the market? If not, says Kuhn, you are probably deluding both yourself and potential investors that your idea will ever attract a critical mass of customers.

Second, you should "focus like a laser beam on your customer." VarsityBooks.com has found that customers in the Internet space demand a highly personalized and value-added experience. Running a Web site is not a mass-marketing exercise. All of the hype in the industry about one-to-one relationships with your customers is grounded in truth.

The third piece of advice, directed specifically at CEOs, is to surround yourself with people who are smart and who are not afraid to challenge your assumptions and opinions. No one runs a successful business by imposing his will and opinions on his team.

## Advice to Other Internet Entrepreneurs

- Be extremely tough on your value proposition and ask, Does your idea cure some "pain" that is out there in the market?
- Develop a good advisory board—avoid becoming a start-up that had great ideas and lousy execution.
- Find people who are smart and who are not afraid to challenge your assumptions and opinions.
- Remember, customers and customer retention is king— you can't create profit without creating customers first, and that means focusing on value and service.

## GATHERING EXPERT ADVICE

Something else Kuhn and his colleagues have learned is the importance of a good advisory board. There are so many horror stories of start-ups that had great ideas and lousy execution. A strong advisory board of technology and business experts dramatically increases the odds that a start-up company will grow and thrive, especially in the new Internet economy. A good advisory board helps a company remain focused on delivering on its value statement. VarsityBooks.com believes that it would not exist today without the help of some smart advisers.

## Bottom Line: Is VarsityBooks.com Profitable Yet?

To date, no. However, Kuhn counsels new Internet businesses to rank retention of customers and valued employees far ahead of profit as indicators of the company's potential. With the economy at a point of major transition right now, the amount of money companies need to invest to compete at the next stage—what Kuhn calls "the Internet stage"—means that profitability is, for the time being, a secondary indicator of a company's worth. He cites Peter Drucker as saying, "There is only one valid definition of business: to create a customer." Kuhn extrapolates this thinking to the current situation in the dot-com world. "We are here to create customers. We can't create profit without creating customers first. And that means we need to focus on value and service. The second important person in this equation, after the customer, is the skilled employee. Without that person, offering value and service are impossible."

## DEFINING THE ROLE OF THE CEO

What about keeping up with industry developments? How does a CEO of an Internet start-up recommend keeping on top of things? Kuhn reads three newspapers a day: *The Washington Post, The New York Times,* and *The Wall Street Journal.* He also reads *The Industry Standard* and receives news stories from college newspapers all over the country through the U-wire. On his reading list as well are *Upside* and *The Red Herring,* and some twenty or thirty Web sites (business- and venture-related, as well as a few of the interactive trades) that he has bookmarked online and browses while he's on the phone or has spare time. He reviews industry headlines and looks regularly at TheStreet.com.

What Kuhn doesn't do as CEO is try to keep abreast of all of the technological developments. While he does read many trade publications that help him keep up with technology, he relies on the company's IT staff to make the best decisions for the business. His time is better spent doing other things.

No day is typical, Kuhn says, but they all seem to start early and end late. Marketing, new site capabilities, the campus representative program, and the company's partnership program are all going full tilt and require a great deal of time and attention. Much of each day is consumed with meetings (with lawyers and external partners) and interviews with media and analyst firms interested in getting to know the company better. Then there are speaking engagements in front of industry groups and interviews (several times a week) with job candidates. On top of that, Kuhn reviews dozens of resumes each week and deals with issues common to any start-up business: office space, facilities, and employee benefits. Then there is all the e-mail to answer.

He needs to stay in touch with his coworkers, too. "I try to spend time just checking in with people," he says. "It's too easy to shield yourself behind your to-do list and ignore issues such as office mood and morale. But you can't afford to do that."

There are, of course, many rewards that come from

all this work, Kuhn says. Most of all, there's the knowledge that your vision and efforts are transforming an old way of doing something into a new way of doing something. After a stressful day, one of his favorite things to do is look at the feedback that students post on Varsity Books.com's Web site. "They feel the difference, and they appreciate the fact that we are helping them save money and making school a little more affordable for them overall," he says.

Another rewarding aspect of running an Internet business is the relationships you develop. If you are working at a start-up, you are spending a lot of time at work—so much time that the people you are working with become an essential part of your life. Kuhn says he has met many remarkable individuals, and the roster just continues to grow as VarsityBooks.com adds to its staff.

### Vision of the New Economy

Internet-based community applications and "digital exchange," or auction, applications are helping to connect people to other people online, the first through stated affinities and the second through supply-and-demand dynamics. The net effect is creating "a freer and fairer market that's less susceptible to artificial price fixing and profiteering. That makes inefficient markets efficient."

Finally, the student representative network, through which he is helping to employ and educate thousands of college students nationwide, is a big reward for Kuhn on a personal level. "It's gratifying," he says, "to think about the fact that that one idea I had back in the law library of my old firm has created new experiences and income for thousands of people, particularly younger people."

## FINDING ROLE MODELS IN THE NEW ECONOMY

Like his fellow entrepreneurs, Kuhn has many thoughts on the Internet in general. "It's here to stay," he says, "and we're just starting to see the transformations it will enable. I agree with George Colony of Forrester [Research], who said that, in relative terms, all of us new 'Net entrepreneurs' are just the very beginning: We're like cavemen sitting around the fire chewing on bones compared to the world that's yet to come."

Nevertheless, Kuhn thinks that there are certain entrepreneurs who are laying the groundwork for that world to come. In particular, he admires Jeff Bezos of Amazon.com. "When the history books get written about this period, he will be recognized as a great American innovator. He was the first to make consumer retail work on a large scale online, and he has continued to grow his service model into other product areas in a way that provides customers real value and community."

At the same time, Kuhn also admires Barnesand Noble.com (even though another division of that company competes with VarsityBooks.com in the textbook space). Barnes & Noble's accomplishment is a different beast from Amazon's. They saw the writing on the wall, Kuhn says, and knew that even though they were successful in their brick-and-mortar business, they had to fundamentally change in some ways. Even though it's been fashionable to knock them and elevate Amazon.com, it's important to keep in mind that in the total scope of things, the Barnes & Noble people were early movers, too. In some ways, it may be harder to change a successful established business than to start one from scratch, since such a business can't operate in the red the way a well-funded start-up can. In addition, their site continues to get better; he looks at it all the time.

Because today's technology is all about entering into a one-to-one relationship with customers (and providing a service or product that resonates on a personal level), Kuhn also has tremendous respect for Dell Computers. Dell has done this better than almost anyone else by allowing customers to configure their systems online before they ship. "Their success has been astounding, and their site offers computer buyers a pretty compelling experience at the same time," he says.

Two final companies he admires are Cisco Systems and AOL. Unlike the aforementioned companies, Cisco isn't a pure-play Internet company per se, but it did something quite interesting in response to the Internet revolution. Cisco elevated itself from the world of routers and hubs and became "the Internet company," positioning itself above the market as the great technical enabler. The reason he admires AOL is because of its focus on its customers. AOL has had its share of ups and downs, but because it makes every decision based on how it will improve the lives of people across the world, it remains a leader. It's a company that never loses sight of its core business and that has been relentless in its efforts to dominate its market.

The experiences of all of these companies, including VarsityBooks.com, get at the heart of how the technology is changing everything. The Internet removes geography as a limitation and gives any consumer anywhere access to the best price and service available for a given product. "That brings choice to everyone online," Kuhn explains. "That creates a freer and fairer market that's less susceptible to artificial price fixing and profiteering. That makes inefficient markets efficient."

Two areas that Kuhn thinks are critical to the new Internet economy are community applications and "digital exchange," or auction, applications. Both are about connecting people to other people online, the first through stated affinities, and the second through supply-and-demand dynamics. These applications have just begun to illustrate their potential, but together they have the ability to transform our culture and economy. When the Web provides the means for people who share a certain interest, opinion, or problem to communicate, new communities spring up in a way that they can't when experience is bound by region and geography. Economically, digital exchange capabilities have the potential to create a more pure supply-and-demand–based economy that is less subject to unfair price fixing and profiteering. "Both [community and auction] technologies have a leveling and liberating effect and will create lots of opportunities for people to communicate across borders, age groups, and social class," says Kuhn. Thus, Kuhn and his colleagues at VarsityBooks.com view the Internet phenomenon as akin to the innovations in electrical and steam power that brought about the Industrial Revolution. They believe that tas he Internet will transform the ways we communicate, locate information, conduct business, and create value.

There's only one thing about the Internet that Kuhn believes has been hyped up: "[It's] people thinking there is something new and radical about the letter *e,* as in e-tail or e-commerce or e-business." As people are getting more and more comfortable shopping for goods and services online, the novelty is wearing off—just as business leaders are all concluding that they need to confront change and build new strategies or they will be obsolete.

# 4

# Enews.com

*The story of how Enews.com became one of the most trafficked sites on the Internet and secured a $20 million investment from Madison Dearborn Partners*

Enews is the leading magazine retailer on the Web. It is consistently ranked among the most visible Web advertisers and is a leading online marketer.

The site debuted in July 1993 (two full years ahead of Amazon.com). Then called the Electronic Newsstand, it featured sample articles and subscription opportunities for eight magazines. Today, Enews offers more than 800 magazine subscriptions in twenty-five categories and over 100 special interest areas for up to 80 percent off the cover prices. With a $20 million investment from Madison Dearborn Partners, a Chicago venture capital firm, Enews, which is headquartered in Washington D.C., has about 50 employees and expects to hire several more within the next six months.

## Coming Up with the Idea

Enews might be the real Amazon of the Internet, having launched more than six years ago (an old-timer by Web standards) as a modest experiment in the electronic distribution of magazine-related promotional material. From the beginning, its owners wanted Enews to become "the ultimate magazine site"—they just weren't sure how. Electronic commerce barely existed in the early 1990s, so the site started as a content provider for publishers. It later evolved into a content site with articles about the magazine world. After Brian Hecht became president and CEO in 1996, the company made the transition to magazine retailer. This model proved effective, and since then, Enews has experienced extraordinary sales growth.

## *Fast-Track Facts*

| | |
|---|---|
| **Key Executive** | Brian Hecht, president and CEO |
| **Business model** | Online retailer (magazines) and direct marketer |
| **Funding** | Madison Dearborn Partners and Clark Estates |
| **Business Affiliates/Partners** | MSN Shopping, CNN Interactive, Disney, to name but three in the 25,000 network |
| **Technology Partners** | BeFree, Frontier GlobalCenter, Vignette Corp. |

The first and crucial step in the company's success since 1996 was its business model. Its owners are Madison Dearborn Capital Partners and Clark Estates, of which Martin Peretz, publisher of the *New Republic,* is a major shareholder. Hecht and Peretz knew each other from Harvard, and both men also knew the magazine industry. The numbers were huge—domestic magazine sales totaled $7 billion in 1998. Hecht and Peretz also discovered that of all magazine sales, 82 percent are made through subscriptions and only 18 percent through single-copy purchases. Furthermore, projections were that Internet commerce would be a $3.2 trillion market by 2003.

Not only were magazine sales big business, the Web seemed the perfect venue to promote them. Unlike traditional newsstands, an online retailer could stay open twenty-four hours a day, seven days a week. An electronic newsstand would also be capable of displaying thousands of magazines, not just what a typical newsstand can hold. It could also provide publication schedules and a detailed description of what each magazine is about.

Most important, if it could deal directly with publishers, it could offer subscriptions at deep discounts— and could earn a commission on every subscription it sold. Unlike brick-and-mortar companies, it wouldn't need an inventory and could avoid the accompanying overhead costs.

## HONING THE MODEL

Since it started selling magazines online, Enews has experienced dramatic quarter-to-quarter growth. By the end of 1998, it had forty-three employees; today it has over 100 and continues to hire. The company is also in the middle of a major marketing push to increase the number of titles it offers from 820 to 20,000 and to boost its number of affiliate partners from 25,000 to 100,000 by the end of 2000. Not surprisingly, Enews has been hailed by *The New York Times, USA Today, Investor's Business Daily,* and *Newsday* as the key player in the fast-growing world of online magazine sales.

What distinguishes Enews from so many other Internet start-ups that never moved beyond an initial good idea? First, Enews guarantees the lowest authorized prices on the Web. Customers can save up to 80 percent off the cover costs of magazines and get a free subscription if they can identify a lower price online.

Second, the site connects shoppers to their favorite magazines through thousands of marketing partnerships: It is the exclusive magazine seller on Yahoo!, Excite, Lycos, Tripod, WebCrawler, and BarnesandNoble.com. It has also made itself one of the most visible retailers on the Internet by establishing an affiliate program with more than 25,000 independent Web sites that sell Enews magazines to their users—and earn cash with every sale. These affiliates include MSN Shopping, CNN Interactive, and Disney. These Web sites—as well as smaller e-commerce merchants, individual home pages, and special interest sites—choose the magazines they want to offer from Enews.com's list of hundreds of titles, and Enews takes care of the rest: order taking, payment, fulfillment, and customer service.

Third, Enews uses the unique capabilities of the Internet to tailor information to individual users and offer them many more services than the traditional newsstand can provide. Customers can search for more than 1,000 magazines by name and subject; browse for magazines in twenty-five categories and over 100 special interest areas; and consult a "Magazine Matcher" to find the perfect title for their interests. They can also buy gift subscriptions through a gift center, sent with a personalized card, and visit a "Help Desk" for shopping guidance. The "My Magazines" section provides information about customers' accounts, allows them to change their address for all of their magazines in one step, and offers special magazine deals catered to their interests.

Finally, Enews strives to differentiate itself from the competition. One of the main ways it does this is by providing original content. Visitors to Enews can buy magazines, but they can also read interviews with magazine editors, summaries of magazine articles, and features stories about what's going on in the industry. Content is linked to other Web sites, including Jim Romenko's MediaGossip.com. Not only does this content bring more people to the site and attract repeat visitors, it also serves as a promotional vehicle.

But perhaps the primary reason Enews stands out from the competition is that it was the first mover of magazine subscriptions on the Internet. Thus it has an established customer base and the largest market reach through its partners and affiliates. Traditional magazine agents have had a difficult time trying to compete because they lack the first-to-market edge and Internet marketing expertise. Other e-commerce vendors have chosen to become partners with Enews rather than try to compete, since selling magazine subscriptions requires a large network of authorizations from hundreds of magazine partners, which is difficult to duplicate.

Yet even though Enews is the number-one magazine retailer, it knows it can't take its position for granted. As CEO Hecht says, "That's why we're constantly working on creating strategic partnerships, reaching out to affiliates, upgrading our site, creating more content on our site, and adding to our list of magazines we offer."

## Enews.com's Key Success Factors

○ Strategic partnerships, including an extensive network of magazine partners that's difficult for competitors to duplicate, marketing alliances, and technology partners
○ Customer service excellence
○ Continual enhancements to its e-commerce infrastructure and technology
○ Permissions-based direct e-mail marketing and offline brand advertising
○ Low employee turnover

## GETTING CAPITAL

Finding financing for Enews has been and no doubt will continue to be "an interesting process," as Hecht puts it. Finding funding remained fairly hard for Enews.com for a long time, and then got easy fairly quickly. That turn in the tide corresponded to an inflection point in the growth of the company.

This is how Hecht explains it: With any given company, the business grows to a critical mass, and there are certain levels of funding that are appropriate for each stage along the way. "Basically, if you're a start-up with little revenues," he says, "then your strategy for approaching venture capital is you have to focus on all the potential, on everything it's going to be. Oddly enough, it's almost better to have no results and be all-potential when it comes to seeking investors."

Acquiring capital is easiest at the very beginning and then later, just before the company goes public—imagine the process as a "sort of a drooping laundry line." In the beginning, there is nothing to disprove your theory. "You can say, 'I'm going to run an Internet company that paints the sky blue, and everyone says, yes, that's a good idea,' " he explains. At that point, no one sees a reason why the sky shouldn't be blue, so people think your company is going to be a great success. Then, at the other end of the laundry line, when it's clear that your company is going public, a sort of valuation occurs. When a company prepares for an initial public offering (IPO), it offers private investors the opportunity to come in and buy at a discount to that valuation. "So it's sort of an easy buck for the venture capitalists, with relatively little risk," says Hecht. Therefore, it's easy for a company to raise capital at that juncture.

After the company has raised some money and has some operating results, it goes out for the next round of funding. For Enews, it was difficult to find financing at that point. The company was in an odd spot, straddling its potential and what it was actually doing. It had its entire infrastructure in place, but not a lot of revenue. "Theoretically, because we were actually doing what we set out to do, it should have been a benefit in terms of seeking financing," says Hecht. But since the company's revenues were mostly based on direct marketing at that stage, money was being spent in order to generate those revenues. Hecht tried to raise capital for almost six months without the assistance of an investment banker but was unsuccessful. "It's not that everyone needs an investment banker," he says, "but if you're new to the experience, the investment banker helps shop you around and lends you credibility and legitimacy."

Before hiring an investment banker, Hecht would go to the investors and owners of Enews and ask them for recommendations of venture capitalists that he could talk to. They would give him some names of contacts and, almost out of professional courtesy to the company's owners and investors, these contacts would meet with him. "I would give them my spiel," Hecht says, "and they'd basically pat me on the back and say, 'Nice company, kid, why don't you give us a call when you know what you're doing?' " Eventually he worked up enough courage to ask the owners to hire an investment bank to help the company raise venture capital. "In some ways, I risked insulting them because it was as if I was saying their references weren't enough," Hecht says. "They were extremely proud of their connections, but they weren't sufficient to get us what we needed." Fortunately, the owners and investors weren't insulted and didn't reject the idea, though they remained somewhat wary because investment bankers are expensive, and they take a cut of whatever money Enews would raise.

Once the investment banker was hired, Hecht was warned that he would be taken through a hellish process. He should expect to meet with maybe sixty venture capitalists and be lucky to receive even one term sheet (investor terms) out of all of them. "But it turned out just the opposite happened," says Hecht. "I loved going out and meeting people. I met about twenty people, not sixty, and received two or three different term sheets that we had our pick from. It was delightful."

Each step of the process did take a little longer than expected, however. Word on the Street is that the first round of financing for a start-up should occur in a tight six- to eight-week time frame: You prepare your proposal for the first two weeks, spend the next three weeks on the road, then close the deal within the last two weeks. Yet in Hecht's experience (and those of people he knows), it never happens quite that way. For Enews, "in some ways even the abundance of interest actually dragged out the process, because now, instead of experiencing a dearth of interest, you have competing elements who want to put in different terms that you have to consider." Admittedly, this was a good problem for the company to have, and Hecht says that "once we became good at telling our story, and once we learned how to talk to the potential investors in a language that they would understand, it became relatively easy."

The hard part, in the case of Enews, was the second round, or the "mezzanine round," of raising venture capital. That's when you're in the middle of the clothesline. "You're beyond the promise and you're beginning to see the results, but often you don't have the resources to make the most of the idea yet, so you're stuck in sort of a catch-22," says Hecht. This is a time when management becomes particularly important; management must continue growing the company in order to sell it to investors. It's also the time when you realize why the first round of financing is critical; the first round must help lay the groundwork for subsequent rounds of raising venture capital. Hecht advises that venture capitalists need to look at the long haul, and even if there is a speed bump in the road between the first round and second round, you want investors who'll stick with your business idea and "understand the big story."

"If the big story hasn't changed, [venture capital investors] should go up to bat with you, put up some more money, and certainly help convince others in the venture capital community to go out on a limb with them," he says.

In the end, Hecht believes how easy (or not) it is for an Internet start-up to raise money depends entirely on the company. There is venture capital out there for the taking—venture capital that's chasing too few good ideas. There are also many Internet ideas out there chasing too few good venture capital dollars, "so what you have is a perceived scarcity from both sides," he notes.

Of course, to those Internet start-ups, everyone's money is green. But Hecht cautions new companies to make sure they look for certain qualities in a venture capitalist:

- Does the VC investor or company have any value-added benefits? For example, can they help you get strategic deals in your market?
- Can the VC help you attract and attain key management?
- Are they honest and good people? Are they going to be good advisers for you? Are they in it for the long haul or are they in it for the quick buck?

When Hecht was looking for capital, he found that the number of Washington D.C. firms that met all those criteria were few and far between, but he acknowledges "it's probably the same thing when they're looking for Internet companies. What's nice is that the result is an efficient market system. The good capital finds the good Internet companies and the good Internet companies find the good capital."

---

### Advice to Other Internet Entrepreneurs

There is venture capital out there for the taking, but if you're new to raising VC, an investment banker can lend credibility and legitimacy.

Cater to the needs of the customer, and turn bad customer experiences into good ones in order to breed customer loyalty.

---

## KEEPING THE CUSTOMER HAPPY

One of the things Enews considers key to its success is its customer service. Customer care representatives answer any and all questions a customer could possibly ask. "They are fully empowered to make every contact a successful one," says Hecht. The subjects of most questions are obvious: "I have not received my magazine. Where is it?" "When can I expect my first issue?" "How can I renew, cancel, or change my address?" The customer care group responds to every e-mail within twenty-four hours of its receipt, with most responses made before the end of the same business day. This amounts to approximately 150 responses a day, a very good rate by any standard.

Even those customers whose questions aren't predictable receive friendly and timely responses. One woman wrote an e-mail asking where she could buy an automatic kitty litter disposal system she had seen advertised on TV. Though the query had nothing to do with Enews and its business, the customer care representative who received the e-mail researched the question and responded with the same energy that he would use to respond to a customer buying magazines that Enews did not carry that item. The company's philosophy: consider anyone with any question as a potential buyer.

For Enews, customer satisfaction is vital to the organization. Sometimes, representatives do everything possible for a customer, but there is nothing that can make the experience a good one. Bad experiences are remedied as quickly as possible with the company sending the customer a token of goodwill—a sweatshirt or mouse pad, for example—fast. The customer care center also has an internal grading program for incoming calls. It's a thirteen-point scale, from A+ to F. Representatives use the program to grade their own experiences. (It is not used for performance review.)

The focus is not on the cost per contact. The company understands that its customer care operation is expensive. It wants to carve out its spot and to be known as the premier magazine retailer on the Internet, and it believes that will happen as a result of the company' s success in marketing and customer care. Its research shows that people will return to the place where they made their first purchase online. Experience and loyalty win in the Internet business so far, and by turning its few bad experiences into better experiences for customers. Enews believes it can breed customer loyalty.

Enews concentrates on strong interpersonal skills when hiring customer care representatives. It wants customers to feel that someone is on their side. Good writing skills are valued. Editors create templates around specific questions that come up often, but representatives often fine-tune the responses or add something to make them more personal.

Highly trained customer care representatives also provide a feeder-pool to other areas of the company. It is difficult to find trained, intelligent people to work as designers, technicians, or marketers. Currently, all customer service representatives have college degrees, and two of them have advanced degrees. Enews does not hire individuals if it does not believe they could advance into other areas of the company. Though the customer care representatives are entry-level employees, they usually make the transition to other departments, in many cases just four to six months after hiring. While no promises are made about advancement, people understand their opportunities when they are hired. Because there is no hierarchy in the customer care environment at Enews— managers do everything from "managing" to entering data to taking phone calls—these employees achieve a good understanding of the company's history and culture. This focus on growing in-house talent helps fuel the company's growth.

In 1998, customer care was handled on a part-time basis. Then a manager of interactive services and a company vice president made the positions full-time. As a result, demand and sales have increased.

## GETTING THE NAME OUT THERE

Marketing deals are another key to success, driving the business. Relationships with Yahoo! and other portals

provide millions of daily users with direct access to
Enews through highly targeted links, buttons, and banners based on keyword and category searches. Partnerships with proven e-commerce destinations such as
BarnesandNoble.com go a step further by allowing Enews
to reach Web consumers already in "shopping mode."
These e-commerce sites also include Cendant's NetMar-
ket, FreeForum, and CoolSavings.com, all of which have
cobrand arrangements that integrate services from
Enews seamlessly into their systems.

The affiliate network is another way to promote
Enews. Niche sites can use an easy-to-set-up program to
customize their own newsstands with a selection of magazines tailored to their users' interests and receive a commission for each magazine sold from their site. Affiliates
include not only large retailers such as Disney but also
specialized merchants such as GolfOutlet.com, PetMarket.
com, Classicpickups.com, and Teen.com. There is also a
special fund-raising program for not-for-profit organizations and school groups.

Enews often works with publishers to develop special online marketing programs as well. For example,
Enews was the exclusive online promoter for the launch
of *Talk* magazine, whose publishers then had access to
the site's extensive market reach on the Web.

Direct marketing is a whole other tack. Enews works
with several companies, such as Excite-owned Match
Logic, to distribute targeted e-mail offers to Web surfers
who have granted permission to receive e-mails corre-
sponding to particular interests. Hecht is a big fan of online promotion. Today, he says, with the use of portals
and key searches, customers are instantly directed to sites
where they are likely to buy what they've been searching

for. Direct marketing through e-mail is both effective and cheap, and databases allow sites to collect data about the spending habits of consumers and what they're looking to purchase.

Even so, Enews is considering using more traditional advertising to increase the company's visibility and to ensure that the pubic is aware that its consumer brand name, Enews, is trademarked and protected. It already reaches new customers through direct mail campaigns and some offline brand advertising. But Enews also tested a new sixty-second radio spot by agency Lawrence Butner that aired in New York City and Washington D.C. area stations and launched a recent national direct mail campaign that targeted people with Internet-shopping experience.

Enews does not, however, carry ads on its own Web site. "We're about selling magazines, so there are no banners for other products," says Hecht.

## MAKING THE MOST OF TECHNOLOGY

Enews relies on major business partners that help maintain and enhance its e-commerce infrastructure. BeFree, the leading provider of online affiliate marketing technology, services, and knowledge, plays a critical role in the ongoing growth of the affiliate program. Frontier GlobalCenter provides Enews (as well as many other leading Web destinations) with redundant direct connections to major Internet backbones, which ensures that customers have nonstop access to magazines. Enews has relied on Vignette Corp. for years to provide its Story-Server Web content application system and continual enhancements to its e-commerce technology. The nine-person production staff at Enews also uses Microsoft Access and other intranet Web-based tables to maintain the look and feel of the site. The design staff uses standard graphics programs such as Adobe Photoshop, Illustrator, Fireworks, and Macromedia Flash to produce graphics for the Web site and for print work as well.

Enews has also recently rolled out Acuity technology to enhance its online customer services. This product allows a single customer care representative to have multiple online conversations at any point in time.

From the end user's perspective it works as follows: A button appears on the site when customer care is available. The customer clicks the button and a chat window pops up. One customer might type in, "I'm scared to put my credit card online. Is there any other way I can order?" Another might ask, "I don' t see any magazines about felines; can you tell me where they are?" The customer care representative can respond to each of the questions in real time, i.e., via keyboard/chat window. and direct the users' browser sessions to where they need to go. The phone representative, using a graphic user interface and split screen, in effect takes control of the customer's browser. The representative can type the URL for the appropriate page, taking the customer to those feline magazines. The customer then has a chance to browse and can leave the page at any time. The representative can also use the tool to try to move the customer to the shopping cart, sending the customer YMAL (You Might Also Like) recommendations. YMALs are developed based on extensive research into customers' shopping behaviors using data mining techniques that determine which other titles best reflect the preferences of the individual customer or other customers with similar tastes.

## Working at Enews

To understand the work environment at Enews, it helps to first understand the management style under twenty-nine -year-old Brian Hecht. Hecht grew up in Port Washington, New York. His first job ever was teaching piano lessons. While attending Harvard University, where he earned a bachelor degree and served as managing editor of the *Harvard Crimson,* he met Martin Peretz, owner of political weekly the *New Republic,* who was teaching a seminar on campus. Peretz remains his professional mentor. After graduating from college, Hecht worked at NBC News in London and then at ABC News on "Turning Point" in New York. He also helped launch *Swing,* the acclaimed magazine for twentysomething readers.

The biggest break in Hecht's career came when he was asked to become the founding editor-in-chief of Tripod, one of the Internet's first and largest community sites. He also served as the online editor of the *New Republic*. In 1996, he joined Enews as the CEO. A self-proclaimed magazine junkie, he's a devoted reader of *The Industry Standard,* the *New Republic,* and *Folio,* among other publications.

Every day is different as the CEO of Enews. Some days Hecht spends part of the day on the shuttle to and from the office in New York City for meetings with his staff. When he's in D.C., he spends a great deal of his time either on the telephone with other e-commerce executives or in meetings with staff members. Since there are no set office hours, the office occasionally goes home with him. He often has conference calls with investors at odd times, whenever it's mutually convenient, sometimes even at midnight.

Hecht tries to make the office environment casual and social, possibly because he knows firsthand that the demands of Internet work make it difficult for driven people like him to find free time in their schedules. "The best ideas occur when you're all hanging out at 9:30 P.M.," he says. That's why he's been reluctant to start a telecommuting program at Enews, although the subject has come up repeatedly. There is no dress code at Enews, and so far good judgment has prevailed and no one has had to be sent home for inappropriate attire. A playful environment— Nerf gun fights and Christmas lights strung from the ceiling throughout the year—helps to relieve pressure. The company maintains a balance of work and fun first and foremost by hiring socially active people who can engage with their coworkers at parties, softball leagues, social hours, and birthday celebrations. Camaraderie is important, especially since work demands and hours have Enews workers spending so much time together.

In Hecht's opinion, the environment of an Internet start-up is different from that of other companies. "First of all, there is a healthy disdain for the status quo," he says. "Perhaps it was a little bit exaggerated in the early days of the Internet, when people would come in wearing no clothes, no shoes to work, and if you weren't spending time at your desk playing video games, then you weren't cool." That kind of rebellious, anarchic company has died down a bit. These days, he says, "One of the marks of pride is being able to . . . compete [in the world of serious business]—but at the same time, you don't want to do what your father was doing. You don't want to be a company man. Companies such as ours consciously strive for points of differentiation, whether it's free Surge in the refrigerator, happy hours with increasing frequency, free metro passes, or Starbucks coffee in the company kitchen."

As a CEO, Hecht realizes that differentiating your company in those types of ways and creating a fun environment is necessary simply to stay competitive in hiring. "It's also been long, long ago proved that people who are psyched to go to work in the morning do better work," he says. "The cost-benefit of what people used to call wasting a bit of time, lounging around or chitchatting around the espresso machine, is an investment back in the company, especially in an environment where some people work twelve-hour days. . . . Things [that make the workplace a little less stressful] are considered such a given at Internet companies, and yet it's so alien to so many people in old-line industries. I can't imagine a great old company like DuPont Chemical taking a field trip to an amusement park every summer."

## Approach to Personnel Management

Growing in-house talent has helped fuel the company's growth. Enews does not hire a person if it does not believe the person could advance into other areas of the company. Also, creating a fun environment in which to work helps the company stay competitive in hiring. Enews tries to balance work and fun in the workplace by hiring socially active people who understand the significant work opportunities and demands.

## MOVING FROM E-COMMERCE TO COMMERCE

On the other hand, Hecht does see some convergence between Internet companies and traditional ones. In many
ways, they are blending together. "Look at how every big
business in the world is striving to become a dot-com in
one way or another," he says. "Now we're realizing that
. . . five years from now, there will be no e-commerce, just
commerce. Which means that everyone will be playing on
the same playing field.

"We've created a nice little playpen for ourselves for
the first few years of the Internet, . . . competing on our
own set of standards against each other for who's the best
little e-commerce site. But now, whether it's market capital or sales or, hopefully, profitability at some point, Internet companies are becoming the same as the offline
companies—whether it's because they're evolving or buying each other or merging or infringing on each other's
missions. Now we have to start playing like grown-ups."

However, working in the Internet industry still has
its own unique risks and rewards. Hecht says his biggest
risk is that he could lose his management team at any
time. The Internet culture is one in which people hop
from company to company each year or so, lured away by
competitors with promises of stock options and the
chance to become the next Steve Case or Bill Gates.
Luckily, turnover at Enews has been unusually low,
which has aided in the company's tremendous growth.
Having employees who have stuck with the company
through its growing pains has been a major factor in the
company's success. Hecht hopes that his experienced
management team will continue to stick with him as well.

Another difficulty for Enews is the fact that the magazine industry hasn't caught up to Internet time yet. When you order a magazine subscription, you have to wait four to six weeks before receiving your first issue. That's just a fact of the industry. Enews is powerless to change it. But when people order anything on the Internet, they want it immediately. The company is looking for ways to get around that.

## LOOKING AHEAD

Enews has clearly been successful in attracting people to its Web site. Hecht says it is rewarding to see how far the company has come in terms what it presents and offers its clients, and to know there are many hundreds of thousands of people enjoying the subscriptions they bought on Enews.

The challenge now is to attract those people who are most likely to make a purchase or register as an Enews customer. The company uses a proprietary database-marketing tool that allows it to treat each location where Enews places an ad outside its own site as a unique source. The system then makes reasonable assumptions about the characteristics of the individuals who come in through each source, predicting what individuals want to see, and brings them into the Web site at the appropriate location.

For example, if someone is doing a Yahoo! search for information about cats, he or she types in the search word "cats." Enews purchases both banner and button locations on the search word "cats," so the search results page displays a banner that reads, "Looking for cats? We have magazines about cats. Click here." Between 8 percent and

15 percent of the people seeing that specific banner click on it and come through to the Enews Web site to a unique location in the system—one click away from the shopping cart.

Because consumer behavior in buying magazines is completely different from most other product categories, Enews puts significant effort into trying to understand what topics a particular consumer is interested in, and then formulating an appropriate magazine offer. Unlike shopping for books or cars, people don't wake up and think about subscribing to a magazine, and it's not a conspicuous-consumption product.

The key to selling magazines is contextual references. Enews is one of very few Internet sites where people go and reveal something about themselves, their likes and dislikes. Its current customer base is mostly Americans and some Canadians who have Internet access and who have an interest in magazines. The company is still in the exploratory stages of expanding overseas and hasn't worked out a marketing plan yet. However, using databases and predictive technology to track its market should help when it is ready to expand its international reach. Because Enews offers a variety of magazines, it has a variety of customers. Its buyers are about 55 percent women.

In addition to increasing its customer base, Enews is constantly seeking more magazines to add to its selection. The company has vastly increased sales over the past year and anticipates continuing this growth pattern. It is also hoping to offer customers an expedited first copy of their magazine subscriptions in the near future.

On the Internet, six months is equivalent to two years; everything gets outdated very quickly. Hecht says that "plans evolve more than they change." Enews is constantly reevaluating, reworking, and rethinking its strategies across the board. The site has undergone seven redesigns within the last five years. Its staff has nearly tripled as well. From an industrywide investment perspective, Internet stocks may continue to be subject to huge market swings, but Internet companies will be considered mainstream within the next couple of years—especially as both traditional companies such as McDonald's and new economy ones such as AOL continue to find new ways to advance business on the Web, even as more entrepreneurs jump into the Internet pool. Consolidation will continue to happen within market sectors, but there will be plenty of room for everybody.

On a personal level, Hecht says it's difficult to imagine doing any other kind of Internet business at the moment, although he's intrigued by the concept of "incubators," which provide early-stage funding and support for new business ideas. The Internet entrepreneur he admires most is Steve Case at AOL, "not just because he created one of the great Internet brands, but also because he has navigated his company through several treacherous times, when people thought AOL was doomed. His optimism, vision, and focus helped keep the company on the track for success."

As for Internet entrepreneur Brian Hecht himself, he has two pieces of advice: The first is to "experiment, experiment, experiment." The second is to not lose sight of the customer. "Companies are so wrapped up in growing bigger, but they're forgetting how to cater to the needs of the client," he says. "We bend over backwards to make sure that our customers and business partners find working with us to be an easy, helpful, and pleasant experience."

## Vision of the New Economy

Traditional companies such as McDonald's and new economy ones such as AOL are blending together as each continues to find new ways to advance business on the Web. Consolidation will continue to happen within market sectors, but there will be plenty of room for everybody.

# 5

# BuyandHold.com

## *An inside look at building an Internet company that capitalizes on the long-term investing habits of online investors*

BuyandHold.com's mission is to fill a void in the online investing marketplace. The Wall Street–based online broker offers an unusually low-cost service that allows both new and experienced investors to reap the benefits of long-term stock ownership. Users can open an account at the company Web site and start investing online with as little as $20. Transaction fees are $2.99 per order, and investors can consolidate dividend reinvestment plans and direct stock purchase plans into one account.

If the mission is to make investing truly affordable, convenient, and rewarding for everyone, the company's purpose is to help its customers achieve their financial goals through proven "buy and hold" investment practices. In this sense, BuyandHold.com provides the convenience of online access, yet offers a conservative approach to long-term investing by providing greater educational content and a defined list of investment choices. The company provides the services that combine all of the content, commerce, and community the investor needs to make smart financial choices.

## THE PLAYERS

Founder Geoffrey M. Tudisco is only twenty-four years old. Born and raised in New York City, he went to the University of Michigan for college and planned to be an aerospace engineering major. During his second year, he decided to change his major to political science. Social problems seemed more real to him than engineering problems, and he hoped that someday he would be given the chance to help fix them.

But then he got turned on to the world of finance.

Tudisco interned at Goldman Sachs the summer after his junior year. Every day after work, he'd run home and

### *Fast-Track Facts*

| | |
|---|---|
| **Cofounders** | Geoffrey M. Tudisco, Peter E. Breen, and Michael D. Macleod |
| **Business model** | Online brokerage service with vertical market focus |
| **Business Partners** | CNN.com, USAToday.com, the Motley Fool, Quicken.com, AT&T, WorldNet, MyWay.com, Women.com |
| **Target Customers** | Women, parents, and "newbie" online investors |

get on America Online to learn more about stocks and investing. That was also when he discovered the Motley Fool (www.fool.com), which taught him the basics about investing. All of a sudden, he felt empowered. With a little cash to play with from his internship, he opened a Charles Schwab online brokerage account in August 1996. He started by buying two penny stocks—expecting to hit it big—and got burned. One went from about $2 a share to $3, when he sold, but the other went from about $1 to 23 cents, and is even lower now. "One of my first investments got me caught in a good old 'pump and dump,' " Tudisco laughs. "Well, I learned my lesson."

The following fall, he returned to school and continued using the Motley Fool through AOL. The Fool introduced him to a concept called DRIP investing, or investing directly through a company's dividend reinvestment program. DRIP programs are great for small investors who have only a few hundred dollars to invest at a time. They are also excellent long-term investment vehicles. The stocks you can DRIP are all big-name, blue chip companies, "so I thought this is what I should have done with my money in the first place," says Tudisco. "Buy and hold—it may be boring, but it works."

He was so fascinated by DRIP investing that he asked the Motley Fool for more information. The Fool referred him to Chuck Carlson, "who was some sort of expert on the subject and a member of Fooldom [the Fool's community]." Tudisco e-mailed him and got a prompt response with more information and a sample newsletter that Carlson had written. The information came in handy, and Tudisco opened three DRIP accounts and started to invest in them regularly. He continued to buy stock, but only from good, solid companies, through his Schwab account.

After graduating from the University of Michigan, Tudisco took the summer off (deciding to enjoy his last summer before entering the real world), then began interviewing for jobs in August. One of the last interviews he had was at a small firm called Shareholder Communications Corporation (SCC). The firm worked with companies and their DRIP programs and was actually in a partnership with Carlson. "I thought it was rather funny that I somehow knew what they were talking about during the interview, and it seemed to take them by surprise as well," says Tudisco.

One of the things about Shareholder Communications that particularly interested Tudisco was a service called the Direct Purchase Plan Clearinghouse, the only source around that allowed investors to call and request enrollment materials for hundreds of companies that offered direct investing programs. Tudisco, an Internet enthusiast, immediately realized the potential of this service when combined with a Web site. In fact, during his interview, he asked if the service had a Web site. It didn't. "I mentally accepted the job then and there," says Tudisco. "On August 18, 1997, my life—and the lives of two others—were about to change forever."

At Shareholder Communications, Tudisco met Peter E. Breen, who would go on to become BuyandHold.com's chairman and CEO. Breen was actually his boss at Shareholder Communications, and today he is the only person at BuyandHold.com who has been with the company as long as Tudisco has. Breen's background included service as a commissioned infantry officer in the United States Army after college. Then he began a twelve-year career in the securities industry, focusing heavily on the operational and sales functions within the securities processing sector. He started his career in the reorganization department of Oppenheimer & Co., then worked in Mellon Bank Corporation's securities transfer services as an operations manager and relationship officer. His next position was with the American Stock Transfer and Trust Company, where he became a highly successful sales executive. Then he moved to SCC, where he served as senior vice president and partner.

With his partner at SCC, Michael D. Macleod, Breen spearheaded that company's corporate sales efforts and consistently posted the largest sales numbers at the company. As a team, Breen and Macleod worked extensively with members of senior management of many Fortune 500 companies, and they were responsible for acquiring and managing transactions for some of the largest companies in the world, including McDonald's Corporation, the Walt Disney Company, AT&T, Bell Atlantic, and Home Depot. Today, Macleod serves as BuyandHold. com's president and COO, and he shares responsibilities with Breen in developing the overall strategic direction and planning for the company.

At twenty-four, Tudisco obviously has less experience than his cofounders, but he has a proven entrepreneurial spirit. At seventeen, he started Transit Clothing Company as he was finishing up his senior year in high school. His inspiration: the New York City subway system. Tudisco went to the New York County Clerk's office to register the name. Then he started going to the garment district every day after school to learn about the clothing business and talk to embroiderers and silkscreeners about how to make hats and T-shirts. "It was pretty fun, but [that business] cost a lot to start up," he says. "The experience taught me a lot, especially the need to plan a business out in advance and find partners with capital. All of my friends thought the [clothing company] idea was a great one and bought Transit gear from me, but the start-up capital came straight out of my pocket—a pretty expensive lesson to learn at seventeen."

## The Green Light

After his interview at SCC in August 1997, Tudisco was hired as an account executive. His job was to sell the firm's services to corporate clients, but he still had the Web site for the Direct Purchase Plan Clearinghouse on his mind. SCC, he felt, had no idea of the potential the Web had to offer, and he wanted to change that.

Soon after he started at SCC, the firm partnered with a company called Netstockdirect.com to offer the Clearinghouse's service over the Web. "I thought that [decision] was nuts," says Tudisco. "I was not given the green light on a Web strategy to build our own Web site, so instead I studied the revenue model and tried to figure out how to build a better mousetrap."

Then, a turn of events in October 1997 ended up giving Tudisco the ammo he needed to pursue his Web strategy. Netstockdirect.com redesigned its Web site and removed all indications that the Clearinghouse was a partner. "I showed this to Peter [Breen], as the Clearinghouse was his baby," says Tudisco, "and he gave me the go-ahead for the Web site."

Within thirty days, SCC had built Enrolldirect.com, "a sloppy little Web site that proved the concept and excited the company about the potential of the Internet," explains Tudisco. "It did what it had to do," which was to pave the way for the next project, the creation of an e-commerce version of Enrolldirect.com that would allow investors to actually purchase securities online. The question was how exactly to execute this plan. In November, the company got a call from Intel Corp., one of Breen's best corporate clients, that suddenly brought it all into focus. Intel wanted to give investors the ability to purchase shares in the company for small amounts of money, because it wanted to increase its long-term investor base. It wanted to create a direct purchase plan, but it didn't want to pay for the new shareholders. All registered shareholders (i.e., those shareholders who are on the books of a company) cost the company money because the company has to pay transfer agents to maintain an account for each registered shareholder. Direct purchase and dividend reinvestment plans are made up of registered shareholders, and direct purchase plans actually increase the number of registered shareholders, thus costing the company more money.

In the course of addressing Intel's dilemma, Breen and Tudisco discovered their solution to creating an e-commerce Web site where investors could enroll directly and purchase securities. They remembered that SCC owned a brokerage subsidiary, Shareholder Securities Corporation. It did virtually no business, yet would provide the necessary regulatory pieces to enable an e-commerce venture to become a reality. Perhaps SCC could build a brokerage that had the look and feel of a direct purchase and dividend reinvestment plan but didn't cost the individual companies money. This solution would fill a definite need in the market, since direct purchase plans are immensely popular with investors (because they lower the barriers to investing even more than online brokers do). At the same time, it eliminated the unpopular part of the proposition: namely, companies needing to pay the costs associated with such plans. "So we had the solution [for what eventually was named BuyandHold.com] and moved forward," says Tudisco, "but we had no idea that it would take two years to see it become a reality."

The chief obstacle was the reluctance—in retrospect, lack of vision—of the old company, Shareholder Communications Corporation. "They failed to recognize that the Internet was revolutionizing the way business is done, and in turn failed to give us what we needed to make BuyandHold.com a success," says Tudisco. "If we had had their full support from the beginning, BuyandHold.com would have launched in the fourth quarter of 1998. The costs associated with starting an online business are tremendous, so I understand [SCC's] unwillingness to help foot the bill, but they could have said so earlier and saved us a lot of time."

Thus, while conceptually BuyandHold.com began in November 1997, the company wasn't formally started until November 1998. The separation from Shareholder Communications was finalized in February 1999.

Once the separation from SCC was complete, the growth of BuyandHold.com took off. Before November 1998 the company was just two people, Breen and Tudisco, then three people with the addition of Macleod, and five people by February 1999. The company quickly outgrew its two offices on Wall Street in New York City and secured a third space on Water Street. The company had close to 300 employees before the end of 2000.

## THE REALITY

Today, BuyandHold.com, Inc. is the realization of the
founders' dream—an online brokerage that caters to the
needs of long-term investors. Keeping in mind that the
fundamental idea behind BuyandHold.com is to make
long-term stock investing affordable, exciting, and convenient for everyone, the company had some new hurdles
to overcome.

Although millions of investors currently "buy and
hold" through dividend reinvestment plans and other
self-directed investment vehicles, many millions more do
not invest in the stock market at all. They feel they don't
have enough money to participate; they are unsure about
where to start; or they lack the knowledge to succeed
and are intimidated by stockbrokers. BuyandHold.com
needed to build a service that would help would-be investors overcome these obstacles and begin planning for the
future. Everything about the company's Web site is designed to make the investing experience simple. A flat
transaction fee, a minimum investment amount, and an
online shopping cart all help. The company's e-commerce
engine allows users to buy and sell stocks of more than
1,200 high-quality companies or index-tracking stocks
for a flat commission of $2.99 per transaction. The site
also includes an in-depth glossary of financial terms to
educate users. Since BuyandHold.com doesn't require a
large investment, it's easy to get started. It's a relatively
simple process accompanied by lots of online support and
guidance, and it eliminates pressure from a stockbroker
to continually place trades.

BuyandHold.com stresses the importance of education, patience, and discipline with customers. Its found-

ers want to dispel the myth that "market timing" is a wise investment strategy for individual investors. Instead, they want to demonstrate to investors that taking advantage of dollar cost averaging (i.e., investing regularly, with routine frequency, in a particular company with a fixed-dollar denomination), combined with the compounding factor of reinvested dividends, will yield the greatest return for individual investors over time.

The company hopes to take advantage of an expected second wave of the online investing revolution, when the mainstream population comes online, by positioning itself as the online broker for long-term, do-it-yourself investors. Tudisco admires the ability that the other online brokerages have shown in building their brands into trusted household names in a short time. "They began the online investing revolution but let it turn into a day-trading crazed frenzy," he says. "Their services were widely accepted by the early adopters who were attracted by the video-gamelike pace of trading stocks online. We wanted to bring the online investing revolution full circle by bringing a service to market that appealed to the mainstream investor who has a more conservative strategy." Its service will also appeal to millions of customers who currently use traditional brokerages that share the buy and hold mentality: mutual fund investors, DRIP investors, new investors, and noninvestors alike.

The business model that BuyandHold.com has adopted is a vertical market one. By combining the powerful features of commerce, content, and community into an online brokerage service that is unique and highly focused, it hopes to create a profitable niche in one of the fastest-growing and competitive sectors of the Internet. Revenue will be generated through five separate channels:

○ Transaction fees of $2.99 for each customer's purchase or sale of stock
○ Referral fees for products and services sold through the Web site
○ Advertising revenues generated through "brand and positioning fees" for exclusive partners and banner advertisements throughout the site
○ Optional service fees for additional customized services offered by the company
○ Management fees for the IRA feature and availability of mutual funds

The company is considering additional revenue sources that it can create through such new product and service offerings as mutual funds and margin accounts.

### BuyandHold.com's Key Success Factors

○ Focusing on a niche segment (i.e., long-term, conservative investor) within its category of business
○ Online and offline partnerships that provide substantial account acquisition benefits
○ Management team with deep experience in the brokerage industry
○ Listening to the voice of the customer when setting the company's priorities
○ Constant innovation and product development

## THE NITTY-GRITTY MANAGEMENT CHALLENGES

Most of BuyandHold.com's management team came to the company through referrals. This method of recruitment proved advantageous for the company because it filled positions quickly, and many people hired through referral already had some sort of working relationship with each other.

The management team has terrific experience in the brokerage industry, which is crucial when you're starting a regulated business from scratch. "Getting everyone to think in Net terms has taken a little bit longer," says Tudisco, "but everyone has definitely adapted to the speed of the Internet." BuyandHold.com has also found it relatively easy to attract top-notch talent as it has grown (unlike some of the other Internet start-ups profiled in this book). "Now it is time for us to focus on hiring the Young Turks that have been using the technology longer and have all new ideas about how to use the technology to make investing even easier," says Tudisco.

To attract employees, the company offers a combined compensation package of salary plus options and tries to be very generous with the latter. People feel a sense of pride when they own stock in the company. The options also fuel ". . . the dreams of lucrative upside potential," says Tudisco.

More challenging than finding the right talent has been dealing with the legal and regulatory issues surrounding the brokerage industry. Entering the industry was easy, but getting BuyandHold.com's quirky service past regulators was tough, although in the end they agreed that it was providing a service that benefited the consumer. Furthermore, the online brokerage industry at large faces ongoing scrutiny. The National Association of Securities Dealers (NASD) and Securities and Exchange Commission (SEC) are keeping close tabs on online brokerages because of all the customers who have lost their shirts trying to time the market—and the criticism that their brokerages didn't prevent them from committing financial suicide.

## THE IMPORTANCE OF FINDING (AND KEEPING) THE RIGHT CUSTOMERS

Marketing BuyandHold.com has been another challenging proposition. The company projects that it will spend several million dollars during 2000–2001 primarily on print advertising and public relations. "We could easily spend more if we had it," says Tudisco, "but we're looking at more organic ways to generate buzz. The advertising world is so cluttered by dot-coms in general, it is hard to stand out. And the online brokerage space is about as bad as it gets."

BuyandHold.com has entered into numerous partnerships, both online and offline, to solidify its position in markets that are likely to introduce the company to a large pool of potential customers. Current partners include CNN.com, USAToday.com, the Motley Fool, Quicken.com, AT&T WorldNet, MyWay.com, and Women.com. Marketing and public relations programs have focused on media outlets where the clutter of competing messages is either sparse or nonexistent, so as to establish "category exclusivity" and build brand awareness among potential customers.

Consequently, BuyandHold.com has targeted audiences that tend to be conservative when it comes to investing. "We built BuyandHold.com for long-term investors who didn't have an online brokerage that addressed their needs," explains Tudisco. "Peter, Michael, and I are all 'buy and hold' investors, so we had a good idea of what our service should offer. We then identified several primary target markets and conducted surveys regarding our service to determine what features and benefits they found most attractive. We've used that market research to craft highly targeted messages to each specific audience and position ourselves properly in each market while maintaining our core brand position."

Market studies show that three key target markets share a long-term philosophy when it comes to investments and savings: women, parents, and "newbie" online investors. BuyandHold.com has conducted several surveys of its own to ensure that it speaks to the specific needs of each audience and has concluded that the lack of competition is a blessing in disguise. Women and parents want to invest, but other online brokers have not yet figured out how to thoroughly address their needs and therefore do not present a compelling value proposition.

These new online investors need to be educated on the concept and value of online investing. Through its partnerships, BuyandHold.com provides new investors with uncomplicated information to help them get started, without bombarding them with the buy, sell, and trade now craze other online brokers are profiting from. Instead, the company's community offerings contain an extensive library of educational information, expert third-party content and research, tools, and message boards—all of which ensure that its Web site receives a steady stream of new and repeat visitors.

Customer feedback is what determines the company's priorities. It uses customer suggestions and comments to make the service better. "We let our customers tell us what they want. We no longer try to anticipate what they want," says Tudisco. "If we have an idea for a new service we think they'll like, we don't just go out and build it. We survey our customers and constantly ask them for feedback to make sure that we always have their interests in mind.''

Tudisco believes that listening to what customers want, then delivering products and services that address those demands, keeps the company from letting competitors take advantage of its potential shortfalls. Constant innovation and product development will be key to maintaining BuyandHold.com's competitive edge. "We won't rest until 100 percent of our customers are 100 percent satisfied with our service,'' he says. Not enough companies are listening to their customers, he adds—and he's not just talking about online brokerages. Companies are still designing Web sites that are not user-friendly. They forget that a majority of people still access the Web through dial-up connections that aren't meant to handle bandwidth-intensive applications.

Feedback typically gets directed to the company's customer service department. There, a customer service team keeps detailed notes regarding any and all comments regarding the site or the service. Customer service then works with product development to determine what the service priorities should be. Probably the most common feedback the company has heard is that people appreciate the site's ease of use and its simple, clean navigation and design. It is something that many find refreshing.

As a consequence, BuyandHold.com currently owns a niche within its category of business. There are some 150 online brokers out there, but none of them besides BuyandHold.com commits itself to the long-term investor. In fact, many are still wrestling with their identities

and their position in the marketplace. "We have no problem being everyone's second brokerage account, but a lot
of the players in our industry want to be your only brokerage account," says Tudisco. "They think they own
their customers, but in fact their customers own them.
Their customers can pick up and move their account
wherever they want."

Interestingly, instead of other online brokerages,
BuyandHold.com considers its main competition to be
mutual funds, 401-Ks, savings accounts, dividend reinvestment plans, bonds, and any other kind of long-term
investment vehicle.

## Advice to Other Internet Entrepreneurs

○ Don't think you "own your customers"; in fact, your customers own you because they can pick up and move
wherever they want.

○ Recognize that starting up a company is more than a
full-time job; it consumes virtually every aspect of your
life.

○ If you don't have the stomach for conducting business at
Mach 4, then you shouldn't be looking to get involved in
an Internet firm.

○ Hire top-quality people with good organization skills and,
hopefully, some who have started up a company before.
Also, constantly recruit the best talent straight out of universities and colleges.

○ Establish a good technology team.

○ Protect your product or service idea by filing a patent, if
that's an option, so you can then license your product or
service to the highest bidder.

## NEAR- AND LONG-TERM PLANS

The company's plans and strategies have remained relatively unchanged for the last year or so in terms of its key messages and brand identity. Though the management team has created a ten-year plan that looks ahead over the next decade, they constantly amend this plan as projects begin and new ideas surface.

### Bottom Line: Is BuyandHold.com Profitable Yet?

The company is not yet profitable, so at this point it measures success in terms of employee attitude and growth in its customer base. "If people are excited to be here, are working hard, and are coming up with new ideas—and all that is helping attract new customers—then we're successful," says Tudisco. "People here believe in the magic; from what I hear that's hard to find in start-ups nowadays. Employee enthusiasm is high, and we hope it stays that way. Our service has just got this innate, good quality to it that people can understand and say, 'Hey, that makes sense.' "

One key strategy in the company's nearer-term plan is to expand internationally to markets that have similar regulatory environments to the United States. "Long-term investing is not something specific to the American investor," says Tudisco. "As we expand internationally, we are going to continue to stress the importance of investing early on, investing regularly, and building a diversified portfolio." In anticipation of this international growth, the company has built its site to be easily translated into different languages. "Speaking to people in their native tongue will also be critical to our success, which means we'll need to have customer service support that is multi-lingual," Tudisco adds.

As for BuyandHold.com's exit strategies, they are fairly typical: acquisition by a larger online broker or financial service provider or growth to the point that it can do a successful initial public offering.

---

### Approach to Personnel Management

To attract employees, the company offers a combined compensation package of salary plus options and tries to be very generous with the latter. Because the typical day at BuyandHold.com is about ten to twelve hours long, the company provides a free car service and dinner to those who stay late. It also furnishes plenty of toys—Nerf and a daily dose of Half-Life, "that ultra-addictive, first-person, 3-D shoot-em-up game"—both to relieve stress and help people think more creatively.

---

## NO GRAY FLANNEL SUIT REQUIRED

BuyandHold.com's Wall Street corporate office looks as if it got taken over by a college and turned into a dormitory. Tudisco's office is particularly strange. There is no desk; instead, he has a beanbag lounge chair with an ottoman and a two-person beanbag pancake. "It is a comfortable work environment," he says, "and people around the office seem to have taken cues from me.

"I walked into our Web development room the other day and one of our developers was sitting in a beanbag, at his desk, with his monitor tilted down at him, his head-phones on, and his shoes off. I tapped him on the shoulder and said, 'Nice Mike, that's the spirit.' He looked up at me and said, 'Hey, man! You looked too damn comfortable in there, so I decided to give it a try, and I like it!' Now almost everyone walks around with their shoes off, and there are beanbags all over the place."

The founders try to keep the atmosphere clear of typical office politics. They want people always to feel that they can approach any member of management, "so if someone has an idea, they typically share it and know that management is listening to them," Tudisco says. "We encourage our people to come up with innovative solutions to problems or creative new product or service offerings because we need to make sure the entrepreneurial spirit doesn't die, and when possible, we go with their suggestions. Everyone's ego is kept in check because the whole place is full of a bunch of smart-asses, which is terrific," he adds.

Everyone has a lot of fun despite the hard work at hand. BuyandHold.com issues Nerf guns to all new employees "to defend themselves in the event a war breaks out." Stray Nerf bullets are strewn throughout the office, behind desks, cabinets, in the hallways, virtually all over the place. "They help people relieve some stress because you can take a shot at anyone you want. It's a harmless way to blow off some steam," Tudisco explains.

The company is considering adding even more toys to the office that will help people think in a more creative fashion. "Toys are great tools to get the mind working and thinking," says Tudisco. "It's difficult to sit in a room and just think; you need some sort of stimulation, and toys seem to work wonders. People start to play and they get all goofy—and come up with some terrific solutions."

The typical day at BuyandHold.com is about ten to twelve hours long. Everyone does a little bit of everything. Most employees are at work by 8 A.M., including management. The first thing people do is check their e-mail and voice mail to see how the day is going to unfold. Responding to those messages is usually next. Some of these correspondences may be more complicated than others and require going back and forth throughout the day to resolve some issue, but usually they are simple questions or reminders.

With so much going on all the time, there is a need for people to get together and discuss work matters, such as how to position the company in a particular market or, more simply, what the priorities are for the day. An occasional random Nerf bullet hits a window or a cubicle. Lunch breaks up the day and gets people together in the cafeteria joking around and socializing.

The afternoon is usually more hectic than the morning because all of the West Coast is then awake. Luckily, many of BuyandHold.com's partners now have offices on the East Coast, which at least allows the company's schedule to remain on New York time.

Close of the market allows everyone to calm down and make sure all of the day's customers were serviced properly. Some people start to head out at 5 P.M. because they have long commutes. Of course, everyone has the occasional long night, as at any start-up. But the company provides a free car service and dinner to those who stay late. That's when the Nerf guns come out and someone does "an HL check." That's the daily dose of Half-Life, "that ultra-addictive, first-person, 3-D shoot-em-up game," explains Tudisco. At the end of each day, someone usually either fires up a game on the local area network or a couple of people decide to go out on the Net as a team and "just beat up on some other players."

"We get as many people in the company to play as possible," says Tudisco, "though some people prefer to just leave instead of sticking around and getting addicted to HL like the rest of us. It's great because every employee, from our CEO to a customer service representative, is playing and blowing each other's heads off. It's a great tool to make everyone, no matter how new or entry-level [they are] in the company, feel like part of the team." By 6:30 you can hear the explosions and shotgun blasts throughout the hallways at BuyandHold.com, and that pretty much signals the end of the working day.

## WORDS OF WISDOM

Tudisco says the most important piece of advice someone gave him when he was starting his business was to know what you're getting into. "Starting up a company is more than a full-time job; it consumes virtually every aspect of your life," he says. "Many people think it's a lot easier than it is, and fail. Before anyone makes the leap into the startup world, they [should] weigh the risks and rewards."

A piece of advice that he offers is to "hire top-quality people, period. Surround yourself with the best talent you can find; hopefully you'll find some people who have started up a company before, and you will be fine." BuyandHold.com plans to maintain its edge by constantly recruiting the best talent straight out of universities and colleges. The younger generations are going to experience the Internet more and more as part of everyday life, so this new blood will help provide customers with innovative new product offerings that help them better prepare for their financial future.

A good technology team is particularly important for an Internet company. Michael E. O'Dea joined Buyand-Hold.com in April 1998 and made an immediate impact. The company's initial Web development firm built a flawed data model, a fact O'Dea brought to light. He committed himself to rebuilding the entire Web site from scratch. This saved BuyandHold.com from falling flat on its face by launching with an inferior data model that could not support its business. O'Dea brought on a top-notch Web development team that transformed BuyandHold.com into a reality within six months.

Tudisco and his colleagues also advise staying organized and keeping your priorities straight. It becomes difficult to remain focused on what needs to be done when you're pulled in several directions, they say. Prioritizing your "to do" list helps, as does surrounding yourself with top-quality people with good organizational skills. Those people can take more off your plate, thus freeing up some of your time. Good organizational skills help you set priorities and manage relationships with partners and investors.

"People often hear me yelling that there aren't enough hours in the day to get everything done," says Tudisco, "but if you surround yourself with talented people, you'll find that things get done, and everyone can focus more on their core competencies. If you don't have tons of bodies to throw things at, then you're going to have to just work harder and work longer. It comes down to maximizing your productivity. "Time is the most valuable commodity in the Internet economy, and it moves ten times faster than in real life," he adds. ". . . There are so many people out there with wonderful ideas, and if you let your guard down, they'll steal your customers. The pace of innovation and the intense competition keep everyone on their toes. If you don't have a stomach for conducting business at Mach 4, then you shouldn't be looking to get involved in an Internet firm."

Another key to starting an Internet business is to do everything you can to protect your idea, especially if it is for a product or service that is not currently offered. File a patent as soon as possible, if that's an option. As the bigger companies continue to battle it out, new businesses can then license their product or service to the highest bidder.

Strategic partnerships are also crucial for Internet start-ups. This is because they help drive traffic to Web sites and associate their well-known, existing brands with new ones. This helps lend credibility to the start-up when "a potential customer comes to your Web site through CNN.com and then sees that AT&T and USAToday are featured on your site," Tudisco says.

The most helpful resource, however, when it came to starting his business, was common sense. "Unfortunately, there wasn't anyone to turn to with a great wealth of knowledge in the Internet space," he explains, "so it came down to good old-fashioned common sense and research. We had to create our own ties in this space and make a name for ourselves from scratch."

He and Breen also tapped into analyst research, such as that provided by Jupiter Communications, which helped them focus "on the most important aspect of any business that hopes to be a success online: the customer experience and customer service." That's where Buyand-Hold.com believes it has developed an advantage. "We want to be the best at servicing the needs of long-term investors and help them take part in the online investing revolution," says Tudisco. "We think that we're better equipped to deal with the concerns those investors have than our competitors because our competitors have been caught up in the fight for the customers with over $100,000 in assets who trade ten times or more per month. They've lost their focus."

Finally, Tudisco notes the importance of staying on top of changing technologies. He and his colleagues participate in industry associations and trade organizations, "as well as maintain a healthy dialogue with customers." BuyandHold.com's customers tell the company what types of products or services they'd like the site to offer, then the company researches how it can make such services possible. Tudisco also reads *The Industry Standard, Business 2.0, Brandweek, Forbes, Fortune, The Wall Street Journal, Barron's, FastCompany, Internet World, Interactive Week,* and *The Red Herring* regularly.

As for challenges, Tudisco thinks the most difficult part of starting and owning your own business is getting others to listen. " I was lucky Peter [Breen] shares the entrepreneurial spirit," he says, "but we had the toughest time getting people at our old company to understand what we wanted to try to do, or to let us go ahead and do what was necessary to get it done. The sooner you can recognize the fact that no one is going to help you but yourself, the better."

There are, of course, rewards to taking on the start-up challenge. Tudisco says the most gratifying thing has been the raves the company has received from its customers. He and his colleagues have learned that after all their years of hard work and research, their service does positively impact people's lives.

"Day trading has been all the rage over the last few years, especially with the advent of the online brokerage," he explains. "Only a small portion of the public fits the profile of an online day trader, but virtually all the online financial services are built around those individuals. To build a service that everyone can use is what interests us. To see that we're helping people who never invested before or couldn't afford to invest to invest for the first time is quite exciting. The reactions I've personally heard from some people have sent chills down my spine," he says. " 'So, you're the broker for the little guy like me.' Yes! That is exactly it."

## Vision of the New Economy

Advertising will always be a prominent source of revenue on the consumer side of the Internet, but transactional revenues will be the main model in the business-to-business side of the Web. There's also ample opportunity, especially in content, for untapped niche audiences. Massive internationalization of the Net away from American dominance of Web sites is also a trend to watch as some developing nations skip industrialization entirely in favor of becoming information age societies.

## COMING SOON

Unlike many of the CEOs featured in this book, Tudisco believes that the Internet craze will probably only last another two years or so, that the Internet as we know it will be a lot different then. "There are only so many things that the Net makes possible," he says. "People will still want to try on clothing before they buy it. People will not want to buy a Snickers bar online and eat it three to five business days later." Furthermore, he notes that many large companies are currently studying the online space and plan to move into it sometime soon, if they haven't already. He thinks that there will be a gradual slowdown in start-ups over the next few years as more of these traditional companies come online and further crowd the marketplaces.

Nonetheless, he believes that there are still many opportunities in the Internet space, especially in content for niche audiences. The African-American and the gay communities are currently the most untapped, he says. But, according to Tudisco, pornography will always be the leader online (it is one of the only segments able to successfully charge for content), "and if you look at what they've been doing," he says, "then I think we're about to see a big push in broadband content for the mainstream Web surfer." Interactive programming will become a reality in the near future, he says, "and new possibilities should present themselves to entrepreneurs who are ready to take advantage of them."

He also believes that original Web programming will become more widespread, but with limitless choices of what to watch, it will become more difficult to capture people's attention. As the Internet expands to include all of these new people and programming options, there will be a newfound need for search engines and guides to help users sort through what's out there.

As for the online purchasing process, Tudisco thinks

that more dynamic advertising initiatives will make it easier. Within the next few years, expect to see advertising that is more interactive and more tailored to individual tastes. "Banners are a clunky advertising tool that people already ignore; my guess is we'll see more multimedia-based advertisements online as broadband becomes a reality," he says. "Also, don't forget e-mail. E-mail is quite effective at reaching people and maintaining relationships with customers."

The fact that Internet advertising is moving away from clicks-per-thousand (or CPM, as it's generally referred to in the industry) deals to more variable arrangements will make for a more efficient marketplace and will help make Internet advertising more accountable. The promises of targeted marketing have not totally become a reality yet, but he believes that in the future, we'll see more transactional sites striking performance-based deals with content sites to pay for higher-quality visitors (as opposed to the standard CPM approach).

Although he believes that advertising will always be a prominent source of revenue on the consumer side of the Internet, transactional revenues will be the main model for the future—especially when you factor in the business-to-business side of the Web. Few companies will be able to pull off a successful subscription-based model online, he says, because so many consumers are used to free information, and advertising revenue will pay to keep some information free. Only focused, high-quality content providers such as *The Wall Street Journal* have been successful in making the subscription model work.

What's Tudisco's longer-term prognosis on the future on the digital world: "It's difficult to predict what kind of opportunities will be present," Tudisco muses. "With that said, I think we'll see massive internationalization of the Net away from American dominance of Web sites." Some developing nations may skip industrialization entirely in favor of becoming information age societies, for example. The best thing that could happen to the industry "is to somehow give everyone in the United States access to the Internet," he says, ". . . specially since there is still a majority of the nation that has yet to go online."

The worst thing, in his opinion, would be the invention of new regulatory bodies to govern the online industry. "Our industry is already highly regulated," he says, but additional regulation "could create obstacles that no one can even imagine at this time." He also thinks that security is still a big concern as well: "If security on the Net were to be compromised on a wide scale, I think a lot of people would get scared and might get turned off by the Net for a while, or at least conduct less business there."

Among current Internet companies, Tudisco particularly admires those that are working hard at innovating new products and services to stay ahead of the competition. In particular, Tudisco places Yahoo!, AOL (with Netscape), and Amazon.com, "in the Internet hall of fame. In just five short years they've all become household names and made huge contributions to the online revolution," he marvels. "AOL helped make the online world part of our daily lives by bringing access to anyone with a computer and a telephone line. Amazon.com singlehandedly proved that e-commerce was safe."

Then there is Charles Schwab, a company that successfully made the transition from the offline world to the online one. Schwab anticipated that the brokerage industry would move online and made the strategic gamble to meet its online-only competitors head-on before losing too much lead time. It transformed itself into the online brokerage industry leader and provided a terrific example of how brick-and-mortar companies can successfully conduct business online. "I think Schwab's management has done a wonderful job of adapting to the new landscape," he says.

Whether it's Schwab or BuyandHold.com, Internet companies definitely help capture people's imagination, Tudisco believes, and they will continue to attract the best when it comes to recruiting talent because of the potential they offer. "People, especially in America, root for the underdog, and a lot of online companies are viewed as underdogs. . . . The Internet has reinvigorated the American entrepreneurial spirit."

# 6

# Liveprint.com*

## *The story of turning a brick-and-mortar business into a solely Internet-based company that caters to small businesses with the quality and creativity of a large graphic design agency*

As president and founder of an award-winning multimedia design and development company, Rick Steele recognized that people were turning to the Internet for free solutions to common business problems and decided to change the focus of his company. In February 1999, he rebranded what was then Meetinghouse Technologies as Liveprint.com, "the Internet source for small-business marketing solutions." Liveprint.com is now backed by Flatiron Partners, Chase Venture Capital Partners, The Anita Kaufman Family Partnership, Liberty Venture

*Now Kinkos.com.

Partners, Wedgewood Capital Group, Wellfleet Holdings II, and others.

Liveprint.com believes that small businesses want the quality and creativity of a large graphic design agency when it comes to customized materials such as business cards, letterhead, and envelopes that define their business image, but they can't always afford the services of a large design firm. Through the cost-efficiencies and convenience of the Internet, however, Liveprint allows small-business owners to access its easy-to-use design tools to create and order direct these kinds of creative marketing materials. Liveprint also helps with more sophisticated communication vehicles, such as newsletters and Web sites, as well as personalized merchandise such as clothing, hats, and mugs—all materials that small businesses use and distribute, ultimately to help them grow their business.

## *Fast-Track Facts*

| | |
|---|---|
| **Founder** | Rick Steele |
| **Business Model** | Web-based outsourcing service provider; revenue model is based solely on the fulfillment of products and the sale of hard goods |
| **Funding** | Flatiron Partners, Chase Venture Capital Partners, The Anita Kaufman Family Partnership, Liberty Venture Partners, Wedgewood Capital Group, Wellfleet Holdings II |
| **Business Partners** | Onebox.com, Inc.com |
| **Target Customers** | Small businesses and small offices/home offices (SOHOs) |

## MOVING ONLINE

Meetinghouse Technologies was founded in 1994 as a developer of high-quality interactive media products, including CD-ROMs and software designed for point-of-purchase kiosks and the Internet/Web. From 1994 through 1998, Meetinghouse completed more than forty award-winning, personal productivity products for consumer, government, and Fortune 500 clients. As president, Rick Steele managed the financial, planning, and account management staff while overseeing the creative and technical direction of all of the company's projects, which generated over $1.5 million in revenue annually.

Before founding Meetinghouse, Rick was chief multimedia engineer and information systems manager for Science Applications International Corporation (SAIC), where he designed, was architect for, and managed the development of large-scale software applications and multimedia systems for the U.S. government. Steele staffed and managed a multimedia support team that provided graphic arts support, video editing and production services, multimedia development, and user support services for more than 150 users on a multimillion-dollar contract.

It was while working for SAIC that business opportunities related to the Web and interactive media began emerging. The company was then stringing together T1 lines across the country and creating a secure, private network in a government simulation contract. It was obvious to Steele that if this kind of experience was being brought to life in a lab, it would soon be available to the rest to the country. In 1994, he broke away from SAIC and created Meetinghouse and became dedicated to creating interactive applications for the Web, CD-ROM, and other media.

It was after his fourth successful year at Meeting-house that Steele decided to move his company completely onto the Web and abandon all contract work. And after studying dozens of industries and probing emerging opportunities, he and his colleagues decided that serving the small-business customer with print and other marketing solutions represented a compelling value proposition—to both his company and the customer.

Steele says that when he was making CD-ROMs in 1995, he "learned firsthand the evils of the retail marketing channel, whereby the developer gets $3 and the consumer pays $49 for each CD-ROM sold." He realized that it was the distribution channel that was taking the profit motive away from the developer and saw the Web as a tremendous opportunity to bypass that entire system and bring a quality offering directly to the consumer. The Internet enabled him to provide essentially the same product more cost effectively than ever before, thus creating greater value for an indefinite number of consumers. It also allowed him to get instant customer feedback on how to improve his product. And that's when he spun off Liveprint.com.

## BUILDING ON WHAT YOU KNOW

Having run a successful multimedia design and development company, he already had a team of professionals with a vast pool of programming and interface development experience. The skills Steele and his coworkers developed over the years proved critical in making the transition to an Internet-based solutions provider.

Liveprint.com assists those in the small office/home

office (SOHO) market to grow their businesses by offering them a set of Web-hosted applications and a distribution channel for creating high-quality marketing communications pieces. In addition, Liveprint.com features industry-specific advice and resources that help small businesses maximize the effectiveness of their marketing campaigns. "My mission has always been to create compelling, easy-to-use software applications that are productivity- and solution-oriented," says Steele. Finally, through Liveprint.com, he has the opportunity to apply his vision and design skills to his own applications. "Without a doubt, Liveprint.com is a clear example of this and our greatest achievement to date."

### Liveprint.com's Key Success Factors

- Dedication to a fast-growing niche market segment
- Internal customer care department that provides valuable research on the target market
- Focus groups of small-business owners that guide decisions on modifications and improvements to the site
- Strategic partnerships with other companies that know the small-business market and are able to help Liveprint acquire members
- Board members who are actively involved and help open doors for the company

## FINDING A NICHE

Because of quantities of scale, limited budgets, and time constraints, small-business owners are often at a disadvantage when trying to secure professional designs, layouts, and marketing communications advice from traditional vendors. Liveprint.com eliminates intermediaries such as consultants, designers, developers, printers, and production facilities by offering small businesses the free tools they need to develop their own materials quickly and easily on the Internet. Liveprint.com virtually eliminates the time-consuming prepress process. Instead, from a Web browser, visitors use enhanced design and suite-building tools to create an entire business identity kit with business cards, envelopes, letterhead, and even a Web site, all by answering a few simple questions.

In essence, Liveprint.com is a service provider and partner to small businesses. It provides proprietary interactive design and distribution tools and a highly customized user experience and is not merely a vendor or a template-based online print shop. Liveprint.com also features expert advice. Marketing communications vehicles are only effective if they are used correctly, so Liveprint.com provides industry-specific tips, articles, and essential resources on how to use these products strategically when starting, growing, or promoting a business.

Strategic partnerships with several key players, including Onebox.com and Inc.com, further help customers to address other business issues that are critical to the success of their company. Through partnerships such as these, Liveprint.com hopes to develop a comprehensive solution to its small-business customers' challenges.

But perhaps the greatest benefit of Liveprint.com is the fact that its free Internet-based tools and advice and twenty-four-hour support allow its small-business customers to work in ways they are accustomed to, when they want to, which saves them valuable time and money. It is precisely because this rapidly expanding group of small businesses and SOHOs has proved to be self-reliant, computer-savvy, and Internet-active that there is an explosive opportunity for professional, self-service, Internet-based solutions like Liveprint.com. SOHOs in particular are the fastest-growing work segment in the United States. Two million new businesses are started each year. Included in this market are approximately 40 million to 45 million individuals who collectively spend an estimated $8 billion to $12 billion annually on commercial printing alone. Billions of dollars more are spent on desktop publishing and related supplies.

## Advice to Other Internet Entrepreneurs

- Remain true to your customer. "When the difference between you and your competition is only a few letters and a click, every effort must be focused on retaining customers."
- Develop a prototype of your Web site before approaching venture capitalists.
- Remain flexible so you can change the company's strategic direction and product as necessary.
- Gather 60 percent to 70 percent of the facts about any situation in the shortest amount of time possible, then apply a healthy dose of intuitive thinking to the rest of your decision-making process.
- Take intellectual property protections seriously and get legal advice on this matter—for yourself and any third-party suppliers.

## SETTING UP SHOP

Steele says that raising private equity to grow Liveprint.-com was a huge and unexpected challenge. Although he had run a successful private company for four years, he had never needed to pursue venture capital investment. He says that an unknown within the venture capital community, "Liveprint.com was nurtured to its first beta release by angel investors, my own credit cards, missed paychecks, 401-K, and the sale of my car."

Once a beta was developed, however, the company was able to raise its first venture financing. The first round of funding was led by New York's Flatiron Partners and Chase Capital Partners in September 1999, and it was only a matter of weeks before Liveprint.com closed its second round.

Although it took longer than expected for the first round of funding, Liveprint.com worked through the financing process, and its patience paid off. Flatiron Partners and Chase Capital Partners, which came on board for the second round of financing as well, are two of the most prominent names in the venture capital arena. Because of their roles in some of the Internet's most successful ventures, they are known throughout the industry and have opened numerous doors for Liveprint.com.

Now that the site is live and Liveprint.com is associated with some of the industry's most well known and successful "smart money" investors, financing has become significantly easier. The company receives calls on a regular basis from venture capitalists who want to become involved and many times actually has to turn away money—"a position I could only dream about two months prior to the launch," says Steele.

## FINDING THE RIGHT PEOPLE WHO CAN MAKE IT HAPPEN

Prior to the launch of its site and the close of its first round of funding, Liveprint.com intentionally ran an exceptionally lean company. It had fewer than two dozen employees and only one administrative person. Steele felt that to get the product to market, the company needed to throw all of its resources at development and information technology. The theory? Bring in the smartest, hardest-working people to be found and together, they would make Liveprint.com a success.

Steele's number-one motto is to "hire the smartest people you can find and give them room to grow, but hold them completely accountable for all their actions—both the good ones and the bad ones.

"In a company that is moving and growing as fast as ours, there is no other way to conduct business efficiently," he explains. "You have to hire the smartest people you can find and then demonstrate that you have the trust and confidence in them that they need to get the job done and to do it well. This isn't always easy. Given the pace at which the company needs to move, the amount of time employees spend in the office, and the challenges they face, it is essential to find people who are not only capable but also mesh with the culture and understand the company's vision."

Consequently, Liveprint.com uses an extensive and unique interview process, which employees refer to as "The Bridgeland Process." Basically, every candidate, regardless of position, goes through a series of half-hour interviews with a representative sample of employees from various departments and levels. The interviewers then evaluate the candidate based on several criteria, including how well he or she would fit in with the team.

This is a significant commitment on the part of both the employer and the candidate (especially when you are interviewing ten to fifteen people a week), but Liveprint.com has found it worth the effort. The result has been the development of "an exceptional team of smart people who share a vision and have worked countless hours to bring it to life," says Steele. "As tough as I am on my fellow employees, I would lie down on a sword for any one of them—and, incidentally, I have in many cases, as I made payroll from my own means."

> ## Approach to Personnel Management
>
> Rick Steele's number-one motto: "Hire the smartest people you can find and give them room to grow, but hold them completely accountable for all their actions—both the good ones and the bad ones." Liveprint.com uses an extensive interview process that takes a significant commitment on the part of both the employer and the candidate. It also provides incentives such as stock options for all full-time employees; competitive salaries; an equitable vacation policy; paid medical/dental/vision insurance; and a 401(k) plan. Other workplace perks are a casual dress code, weekly happy hours, a fully stocked kitchen, and a "decompression room," a gathering place for employees who need to take a break and clear their minds for a few minutes.

Liveprint.com's current management team is comprised of individuals who bring to the table years of Internet, software development, information technology, retail marketing, and customer service experience. "As with any of the up-and-coming Internet companies," says Steele, "the true power behind Liveprint.com is not our room full of servers or any one line of code." Most of these professionals were hired through "the smartest people" theory; others were found through the assistance of executive recruiters. Regardless of how they got there, however, one thing has remained consistent. The company takes every precaution possible to ensure that its management team shares the same vision and understanding of the industry.

For this reason, programs that provide incentive and show appreciation for employees are taken very seriously. For example, every full-time employee, regardless of position, is granted stock options. A comprehensive benefits package includes competitive salaries, an equitable vacation policy, paid medical/dental/vision insurance, and a 401(k) plan. Beyond that, the company is currently in the process of developing a more complex incentive plan to account for the fact that different people have different motivating factors.

Although not financial or tangible, the company feels that its corporate culture is also conducive to providing incentives to employees. Employees at all levels are encouraged to say what is on their minds. There is a two-way dialogue about everything—planning, strategic direction, product development, and marketing the company. This openness is important for minimizing bureaucracy and enabling the company to move at so-called Internet speed. It's also important in making sure employees realize that they play a role in the success of the company, so that they feel comfortable sharing their thoughts and ideas. "Honestly," says Steele, "we often find that some of our best ideas for marketing, product development, or even business development come from brainstorming sessions with representatives from the entire company."

Finally, as the company continues to grow and add new employees every week, it is committed to making

Liveprint.com a fun place to work. It has a casual dress code, weekly happy hours, and a fully stocked kitchen. Yet it is proudest of its "decompression room." This room, which features, among other things, a pool table, Ping-Pong table, foosball table, darts, and bleachers, is a popular gathering place where employees can get away from the grind for awhile.

## KNOWING THE MARKET

Steele and his coworkers believe that the fact that people have increasingly turned to the Internet for free software (e.g., calendars, fax, e-mail, and personal productivity tools) over the past few years is extremely significant. Viewing software on the Internet demonstrates that people want solutions, not software. The Internet enables users to get daily tasks done without having to purchase, install, learn, upgrade, and relearn software.

Steele wants to be the first to approach the small-business market as a solutions provider with powerful Internet-based tools and valuable business resources. His main motivating factor in developing Liveprint.com was and is the desire to be a visionary with regards to technology, his target market, and the Internet.

For example, Steele and his colleagues know that small-business owners are time-starved. Regardless of the industry, the average small-business person is racing against the clock to do everything: strategic planning and accounting, cleaning the office, buying supplies, servicing customers, and more. Most small-business owners have very little time during the business day to run back and forth between designers, printers, and other vendors to get the look and feel of their logo, newsletter, or Web site just right. As an Internet company that is open twenty-four hours a day, seven days a week, 365 days a year, Liveprint.com is able to help customers on their own time schedule, whether that means 2 A.M. or 2 P.M., Saturday or Wednesday.

"My mentor for six years was Gif Munger, an ex-Navy officer who served in Vietnam," says Steele. "From a marketing standpoint, Gif and I always lived by the rule that you should uncover what keeps people up at night and work like hell to find a way to solve their problems, period; it is that simple. If you can do this just once for a customer, you will have that customer for life. That is the greatest brand of customer loyalty. This philosophy is brought to life in its truest form through Liveprint.com, where 'we are dedicated to solving the problems that keep small-business owners up at night'—how to get more customers and keep their businesses going."

Liveprint.com also knows that, with few exceptions, customers will not pay for content or the use of Internet-based tools. "We have already seen clear proof of the fact that, in general, Web users are not willing to pay for Internet-based content or tools, and this is not likely to change in the future. Liveprint.com, like many other Internet companies, has recognized and accepted this fact," says Steele.

Therefore, Liveprint.com's revenue model is based solely on the fulfillment of products and the sale of hard goods. What this means is that Liveprint.com makes its money—through a mix of fees—when customers use its services to produce or distribute the marketing communications products they created for free on its site—

commercial printing, embroidery, electronic newsletters, and so on.

In addition, Liveprint.com has made a conscious decision not to pursue an advertising-based revenue model. By choosing to forgo this potential revenue stream, the company is making a commitment to its customers to maintain a clean, comfortable, hassle-free work environment.

"With greater frequency, people (both at work and at home) are turning to the Internet for immediate solutions and information," says Steele. "As is demonstrated in recent years by dramatic decreases in click-through rates, banner ads are no longer a novelty [that] call visitors to action simply by their sheer presence."

Nevertheless, he acknowledges that the increasing reach of the Internet is a clear indication that it cannot be disregarded as a viable and necessary vehicle for reaching customers—especially for any company engaging in e-commerce. However, Steele believes that for online advertising to be effective in terms of inspiring Internet users to act, it must become smarter and more targeted. Regardless of its format, he says, online advertising must make maximum use of technology to deliver individual consumers the most personalized message possible. Otherwise, the opportunity and the message are likely to be missed.

Not only does Liveprint.com make it a point to know the small-business market and Internet users in general, it tries very hard to learn about its actual users through its internal customer care department. In fact, Steele feels that the greatest and most valuable form of research the company does is through this department.

For example, once its records indicate that a customer has received his or her order, the company follows up with an e-mail from the director of customer care soliciting input, both good and bad. This enables Liveprint-.com to determine which sections of the site are unclear and to address customers' concerns, as well as to enhance the site and product offerings based on customers' needs.

The vast majority of feedback to the company has been favorable. "Customers and visitors are truly amazed that an Internet-based company can offer such a customized product, which takes into account the customer's industry, stage of growth, and corporate image," says Steele. "We are also hearing repeatedly that people are pleased with the site's ease-of-use and clean, organized look."

The company has also gotten extremely positive feedback regarding the level of customer support it offers (24/7/365 support via phone, e-mail, and Web chat) and its sincere commitment to 100 percent customer satisfaction. Liveprint.com's policy is that customers who are not completely satisfied for any reason can return any product, at any time, at the company's expense. It has found that this policy provides a level of comfort to those customers who might otherwise be leery of purchasing products over the Internet.

Liveprint.com has also gotten to know its market through focus groups, which it has conducted at various stages of the company's development. Participants have been both small-business owners who have never visited the site and individuals who have used it. Liveprint.com says it has gained a tremendous amount of insight from these focus groups and has made modifications and improvements to the site as a result. The sessions have also brought to light some preconceived notions that people have, which the company plans to address both through its marketing campaigns and throughout the site.

Finally, Liveprint.com makes an effort to literally get to know its customers. Its Web site invites visitors to its offices, located in historic Old Town Alexandria, Virginia. Steele says his staff laughed at him when he suggested they extend this offer, but he stands by it firmly. "Our offices are modest but comfortable, and for those customers who are interested, they can see how we work and feel the excitement and buzz of a start-up," he says.

## FINDING ROOM TO GROW

The company's estimated marketing budget for 2000 is $25 million, and this money will extend to all facets of online and offline media. As a new site, Liveprint's goal is to generate traffic by delivering a message to a targeted audience. To create the necessary level of interest, traffic, and attention (and to be generally effective), it knows that a multipronged approach to advertising is necessary.

### Bottom Line: Is Liveprint.com Profitable Yet?

Investors, industry analysts, and strategic partners do not expect Liveprint.com to be profitable in the immediate future. Near-term success is measured on the company's ability to acquire and retain members and customers. At the time of this writing, the company has already achieved one of its major goals by being acquired by Kinko's. At the early seed stage, it has pursued both acquisition and initial public offering (IPO) strategies simultaneously.

Recognizing that approximately 30 percent of any site's traffic comes from overseas, the company is also taking steps to incorporate international standards, practices, and shipping into its site, another important strategy that will help Liveprint grow its customer base over time.

A final strategic consideration involves expansion of the site itself. In recent years, Internet users have moved more and more toward vertically focused sites that provide them with a one-stop shop for their online needs. For example, iVillage is a source for women and has information and products on everything from pregnancy and daycare to beginning a new career or becoming politically aware and active. By providing a broad array of information and services, companies such as this are hoping to create "stickiness" with their online community. Liveprint.com believes that if backed up with substance elsewhere on the site, contests, chat rooms, and bulletin boards can go a long way in encouraging repeat visitors and enticing visitors to stay on the site for longer periods of time. Thus it is currently developing a community-oriented section of its site where small-business people can exchange ideas with others within their industry or in the same phase of starting a business.

Prior to the launch of the site, Liveprint.com made several major revisions to its business plan. Luckily, the management team was able to make the changes relatively easily and start down the new path collectively. More recently, the company's changes have been in terms of the depth and breadth of its target market. At this point, Liveprint.com is wholly focused on developing marketing communications solutions for the small-business market.

## KEEPING YOUR EYE ON THE CUSTOMER

The primary piece of advice from Liveprint.com is to remain true to your customer. Steele says that one of the most interesting and influential business books he has read is *Radical Marketing* by Sam Hill and Glen Rifkin. This book of case studies emphasizes the importance of staying in tune with customers, understanding their needs, and using that insight to make business decisions accordingly. Each of the radical marketers featured in the book has become a success by focusing on the larger picture of growth and expansion, not immediate short-term profits.

Recently, the Internet industry has been bombarded with studies about "abandoned shopping carts" and media reports about inadequate levels of customer service by e-commerce companies. When the difference between you and your competition is only a few letters and a click, every effort must be focused on retaining customers. Liveprint.com believes that the easiest way to do this is to go above and beyond in terms of customer service.

"Personally," says Steele, "I feel this is the most important aspect of our business and, because I am my company's harshest critic, unfortunately, I will never be fully satisfied. However, we have a whole team of people who strive each day to improve the customer experience in a meaningful way, and based on our customer feedback, there is no question that we are on track." For Liveprint, the key to developing and deepening brand awareness is "staying true to our core business philosophy—providing solutions to the small-business community."

"Some of the greatest brands in the world have been created by a company's ability to provide good customer

service and stay true to the company's core philosophies,"
he says. "These companies are in part successful because
they avoid the huge marketing hype and Superbowl commercials, thus focusing themselves on what they do best.
For example, when was the last time you saw a Tiffany's
ad? But you do know what they stand for, correct? Sticking to and delivering on their customer service promise
each and every day with each and every customer has created their brand."

"Companies that do not collaborate and provide extended value to the customer will not be successful and
will eventually disappear," he adds. "Personally, as a
consumer, that would be perfectly fine with me."

Conversely, the companies that will be most successful in taking advantage of the Internet will be those that
get customer service right the first time. Both online and
offline, consumers have grown accustomed to mediocre
service and average quality products, he says. Therefore,
those businesses that can demonstrate they understand
their customers' needs, understand the market, and are
committed to providing quality customer service will be
the ones who will be successful. Online, those companies
that are able to provide a personalized customer experience and keep pace with the rapidly changing medium
will benefit most from all the Internet has to offer.

For example, Liveprint.com is also able to offer a
personalized experience, backed by the highest-quality
customer support, to thousands of customers simultaneously. This would not be possible in any brick-and-mortar establishment, never mind one in one office with
fewer than 100 employees. This is because custom product development, whether it's business cards, brochures,
newsletters, Web sites, or embroidered items, is tradi-

tionally a one-on-one business. If a small-business owner were to outsource development of any of these products, he or she generally would need to interact with an individual—to sign a contract, for example.

Another part of providing a good customer experience is collaborations that benefit consumers. Those businesses that collaborate to provide greater value for the customer will ultimately win; as a result, the consumer will win as well. "I call it the *Miracle on 34th Street* method of doing business," says Steele. "In this classic movie, the in-store Santa Claus referred customers to other stores whenever his store didn't have the products for which the customer was looking. The most successful online businesses, both today and tomorrow, must embrace this concept and provide this extended value to the customer."

The benefits to the businesses are as profound as those to the customer, because the customer came to you for a solution and you ultimately provided it. Even though you did not generate any revenue at that point in time, you gained the customer's trust and, most likely, his or her future business.

## GROWING STRATEGIC PARTNERSHIPS

Almost as important as customer service are strategic partnerships. Liveprint.com believes that these partnerships are and will continue to be fundamental to the success of any business competing on the Internet. Through its own strategic partnerships, Liveprint.com has been able to acquire members and to provide a more comprehensive set of products and services than it would have been able to do on its own. Subsequently, both its investors and its customers are happier.

The company's first business development relationship was with Onebox.com, a unified messaging service that offers members free Internet communications services, including voice mail, fax, e-mail, and paging for both Web and phone. To help users distribute their new Onebox.com number to friends, family, and business associates, Onebox.com customers were offered a free set of personalized business cards from Liveprint.com. Liveprint.com has seen tremendous results from this relationship, including 100,000 unique visitors and 10,000 paying orders placed the first month subsequent to the freebie. In fact, on at least four separate occasions, Liveprint.com employees have been at local meetings or traveling and have received one of these cards promoting Liveprint from people they've never met before.

Another one of the company's early partnerships was with Inc.com, an Internet company devoted to bringing comprehensive, high-quality management resources to small businesses. Liveprint.com has been designated an Inc.com Solutions Provider and is therefore the recommended source for the creation of customized communications pieces. It is also featured throughout the Inc.com Web site in various content areas, including "Marketing" and "Running a One-Person Business."

Moving forward, while Liveprint is today exclusively an Internet-based company, given the success of the "clicks and mortar" model in which other dot-coms are investing in physical assets to complement their online businesses, it is pursuing strategic relationships with various land-based retailers as well. The rationale is to be able to talk to customers whether they are online or offline.

Says Steele: "In my opinion, the Internet companies getting it right are doing so by creating these *keiretsu*-like (networks of companies) strategic partnerships. Never could I imagine the power of these deals until we closed our first one with Onebox.com. [Most significant] at that time was that this deal cost me nothing up front. These are the types of win-win deals upon which the new Internet-centric economy will thrive."

### Vision of the New Economy

While there are many companies providing small-business marketing services, some of whom Liveprint.com overlaps and competes with today, it is not clear who will be its long-term competition over the next year as many companies continue to redefine their online strategies. Two strengths companies will need to survive will be persistence and the ability to adapt to a constantly changing environment.

The best thing that could happen to the Internet would be the continued emergence of open standards and for the government to not regulate electronic commerce and other transactional information entities. Look also for the expanded use of data mining and the application service provider (ASP) model, which will be the next killer application online.

## ADVICE FROM THE CEO

Create a board of directors that demonstrates its confidence in your management team, as well as a willingness to be a value-added business partner. Liveprint.com has found its board members to be absolutely critical to its success. Due to their involvement in some of the Internet's most successful ventures, they are known throughout the industry and have opened many doors for the company. These have created tremendous opportunities for Liveprint.com in terms of strategic partnership, additional VC funding, and access to resources.

Another good idea for those starting an Internet business is to develop a prototype of your Web site before approaching venture capitalists. No matter how well you can communicate your business's strategic direction, goals, strengths, and competitive advantage, you have more leverage and will be taken more seriously with the product in hand.

Flexibility is also important. You must be able to change the company's strategic direction and product as necessary. Liveprint.com found itself making changes to its site, products, and overall business plan as a result of feedback it got from potential investors.

The company's approach is to do its best to gather 60 percent to 70 percent of the facts about any situation in the shortest amount of time possible, and to apply a healthy dose of intuitive thinking to the rest of the decision-making process. "This is the only conceivable way to move fast enough to succeed in this space," says Steele. The Internet breeds speed and encourages risk taking. Try something new and you will be rewarded for trying. "Personally, I see no reason why all companies won't compete more effectively if they can embrace these elements," he says.

Another key is to keep on top of the changing technologies. To do this, Steele says he does two things: "I read and I rely on those around me to read." Every week he reads countless magazines, Internet news sites, e-zines, and Internet newsletters—and it still seems as if he misses vital developments. For that reason, he counts on his coworkers to do their jobs as well. Each person is expected to be fully up to speed on the industry, competitors, and the latest technologies that will help them do their jobs better and faster and will benefit the company and the site.

Finally, Steele advises to never let legal issues drive a business decision. "My wife is an attorney, so I can say this," he laughs, "but the best business decisions do not involve lawyers. Make the business decision and then make sure the lawyers bless it later. If lawyers drive the decision-making process, everything will take too long, be too conservative, and, of course, the attorney will charge you by the hour."

The only exceptions to this rule, he says, are intellectual property protections, both for Liveprint.com and its third-party suppliers. Internet companies should be taking every possible precaution when it comes to protecting intellectual property rights.

## FACING CHALLENGES AND RISKS

Steele believes that regardless of the business or industry, personnel issues and the sense of feeling alone in making difficult decisions are the two greatest challenges when starting or owning your own business. "I care deeply about everyone who agrees to join our 'crusade,' and making decisions that adversely affect those people in any way is never easy," he says. "While my coworkers may never know it, these are the issues that keep me up at night."

The most challenging aspect of running an Internet-specific business, he says, is speed to market. Business on the Internet is like a gold rush—you need to stake your claims fast. There are essentially no barriers to entry; the only measure you can take to keep your company flourishing is strong customer loyalty (along with nominal switching costs for those who do decide to change loyalties, since they will pay more to get set up somewhere else).

Another challenge, already mentioned, is finding financing. "It is difficult to make a general, across-the-board statement regarding how easy it is, or is not, for Internet companies to obtain capital right now," says Steele. "It took me nearly twelve months to raise our first round of venture capital financing before we had a beta release. It took us a matter of weeks to close the second round after the site was live." There are numerous variables that go into raising capital. Liveprint.com learned that while it was essentially peddling the same product, management team, and business plan in both the first and second rounds, having its site live made all the difference. Fund-raising becomes much easier once your product is running and you have demonstrated customer demand. Financiers like to see a few data points on the curve.

The greatest risk to Liveprint.com is the fact that since the site launched, it has had a target on its back. Competitors can easily see what it is doing and with whom. Thus the company operates on the principle that at any time, it has at most a four- to six-month cushion before competitors can replicate its products and services. Even that is a conservative statement, says Steele, since you never know who is going to launch a site tomorrow, next week, or next month.

Because he and his employees must work so fast and so hard, Steele's days are anything but typical—or predictable. However, there are a few things that remain constant. "[I always know that] I am going to work long, hard hours," Steele says. "I am going to receive in excess of 100 e-mails and have numerous meetings a day; and at some point, I am going to feel the anxiety of being on the top of a hill on a roller coaster."

To keep track of his constantly changing and increasingly demanding schedule, Steele puts every appointment he makes immediately into his PalmPilot. He also relies on coworkers to keep him where he is supposed to be, when he's supposed to be there. He also brings his laptop and wireless modem with him everywhere he goes, because he never knows when he will find a few unexpected minutes to answer e-mails or get some work done.

Yet even though it is, as Steele puts it, "a careful and calculated juggling act at times," there is no other place he'd rather be. "This is the most exciting time and place I could ever imagine," he says. "Literally, on the day we were closing our first round of venture capital financing, we had twenty-four hours to make payroll. With a staff of twenty-one people and $600 in the bank, one of my coworkers said to me, 'This is like [being] at the top of a roller coaster ride—you are not sure if you are going to have the ride of your life or throw up.' She was right, and we thrive on the excitement and limitless opportunity."

## MOVING FORWARD: WHAT THE FUTURE WILL BRING

"At this point in my life and career, and in this day and age, I could not imagine life without the Internet," says

Steele. He depends on the Internet for information, communications, products, tools, and efficiencies. He shops, makes travel reservations, gets news, communicates via e-mail, and conducts research on the Internet each and every day. He had his first e-mail account in 1989 and considers it the greatest communications tool of the century.

He believes that in a year's time, the opportunities on the Internet will be virtually the same as they are today, from both a business and consumer perspective. However, he thinks that in ten years, the promise of a truly personalized Internet experience will emerge, and in fifty years, the Internet will be intricately woven into every facet of our communications.

Looking ahead, Steele confides that the worst thing that could happen to the Internet industry (in terms of its effect on Liveprint.com) would be if Microsoft Corp. got some sort of hold on the technology and made it proprietary. "They are pulling out all stops to try to do so now, especially in their efforts to squash Java by not making it a standard component of Internet Explorer 5.0," he says.

In contrast, he thinks the best thing that could happen to the Internet would be the continued emergence of open standards, and for the government not to regulate electronic commerce and other transactional information entities.

The Internet company Steele most admires is America Online. "The opportunities for AOL to make a meaningful difference in people's lives are profound," he says. "For all its quirks and drawbacks, AOL continues to adhere to the basic premise of making it simple—the single reason why I believe it has so overwhelmingly eclipsed its competitors."

As for the most untapped niche on the Internet, Steele believes it is data mining. Internet companies are able to gather endless amounts of information on their customers and visitors, but they don't spend much time or many resources to analyze this data. If they took advantage of the wealth of information that is available to them from logs, Web measurement tools, and customer feedback, they could provide a more personalized, engaging user experience and product.

Another area worth going after is the desktop application service provider (ASP) market. ASPs allow you to "rent" applications, which means that the software lives somewhere else and doesn't have to be installed on your computer. "ASPs are, without question, the next killer application. It is not just about selling things anymore," says Steele.

All of this, of course, affects Liveprint.com. "Those who are our competitors today will not be our competitors tomorrow as we continue to develop our comprehensive set of solutions-oriented products and services," says Steele. "Therefore, while there are many companies providing small-business marketing services, some of whom we overlap and compete with today, it is not clear who will be our long-term competition over the next year, as many companies continue to redefine their online strategies."

Two keys to redefining strategies for online success will be persistence and the ability to adapt to a constantly changing environment. All successful online companies must have these two strengths to survive the next three to five years, Steele asserts.

"As we like to say, 'It's a rocket to the moon!' We see a tremendous number of opportunities for helping small businesses start, grow, and promote themselves, thus creating a loyal customer following. The products and services you see on the site today are truly just the tip of the iceberg. I believe we are making a difference for our customers and providing them with the means to effectively grow their businesses. Having been a small-business person myself for several years, I know and appreciate how difficult [it] can be. What gets me out of bed in the morning now is the idea that we are helping the millions of small businesses across the country to grow. To me, that is very exciting."

*As an addendum to this chapter, we would like readers to be informed that owing to a recent merger with Kinkos, Liveprint.com has been renamed Kinkos.com.*

# 7

# GiftCertificates.com

*The consummate entrepreneur and CEO of GiftCertificates.com takes us through the exhilarating ups and downs to becoming the leading place on the Internet for gift certificates*

Gift certificates are among the most popular gift items, with annual sales of $11 billion in 1998 (between 1 percent and 2 percent of almost every retailer's sales). A recent survey conducted by *Incentive Magazine* found that gift certificates are the second most wanted present by adults, after cash. Jonas Lee, founder and CEO of Gift Certificates.com, which he founded in April 1997, felt that the inherently "virtual" nature of gift certificates— they require no "touch and feel" to purchase—made them the ideal e-commerce product. Gift certificates are not only a great gift, but they are particularly well suited for sales over the Internet.

Today, GiftCertificates.com's mission is to be the first place consumers click when they are seeking to purchase gift certificates, and the first place merchants click when they are seeking to sell them.

The company's primary source of revenue is transactional. It buys gift certificates at lower than face value and then sells them at face value. It's a simple model. "We buy low and sell high, just like they did 1,000 years ago," says Lee.

Through GiftCertificates.com, shoppers can send an ideal present to someone without confronting the common challenges associated with shopping for a gift (e.g., not knowing what to buy, not having enough time to shop, fear of getting an inappropriate gift). Shoppers at GiftCertificates.com can expect a wide variety of choices, excellent customer service, timely delivery, personalized greeting cards, and elegant packaging. Through its marketing partnerships and alliances with leading companies in both the online and offline worlds, the company is creating new revenue-sharing and promotional opportunities throughout the Web.

GiftCertificates.com has distribution and marketing alliances with more than eighty leading merchants, including Saks Fifth Avenue, Brooks Brothers, Barnes & Noble, Eddie Bauer, Chanel, Joan & David, Marriott, Bath & Body Works, and the Sharper Image. Its strategic business relationships include such industry-leading companies as American Express, America Online, Compu-Serve, Prodigy, USWeb/CKS, and LinkShare. In addition to many corporate alliances, you might say GiftCertificates.com has found la dolce vita, signing Sophia Loren as the company's brand representative in TV commercials and as a business partner with a significant stake in the company.

Customers can purchase elegantly packaged gift certificates from any of its long list of merchant companies that GiftCertificates.com then sends to the gift recipient. Recipients needn't be Internet users either, since givers can request either a physical gift certificate that's sent via overnight and standard mail or a digital gift certificate that's distributed electronically via e-mail. The company also provides retailers with private-label gift certificate services, i.e., it does their gift certificates for them.

According to Lee, "Through GiftCertificates.com, customers can purchase an original branded gift certificate from a wide assortment of merchants, as well as choose from a variety of gift packaging and shipping options."

## Fast-Track Facts

| | |
|---|---|
| **Founder** | Jonas Lee |
| **Business model** | E-tailer with a simple transactional revenue model: Buy product low and sell high. |
| **Funding** | SCP Private Equity Partners, Gotham Partners, Trump Group (Williams Island, Florida) |
| **Business Partners** | Distribution and marketing alliances with more than 80 merchants; strategic partnerships with American Express, America Online, CompuServe, Prodigy, USWeb/CKS, LinkShare, and Sophia Loren |

## The Beginning

Lee was born in New Jersey and raised in Westchester, New York. He is the oldest son of a Caucasian mother and a Korean father and has two younger sisters. He received his BA in economics from Brandeis University and graduated with distinction from Harvard Business School. He is thirty-three years old, married, and has no children.

Lee is no stranger to starting his own business. In college, he needed some extra money but, he says, "could not figure out any other way to make more than $7 an hour scrubbing the cafeteria floors. And that was the highest-paying job on campus!" So he started a small pizza delivery service. Four days a week, between 8 P.M. and 11:30 P.M., he and a few guys he hired would walk around campus dormitories with hot pizzas and subs, singing a "Pizza Man" ditty. "Hard-studying or hard-partying students would seek us out for late-night chow," he laughs. "I made over $100 an hour—I've never had more free cash since."

After graduating from Brandeis, "I couldn't get a job," he says. "I had a finance and economics education, but during my interviews with banks, I guess I talked a bit too much about the different ideas I had for new companies. After a few failed interviews, I took matters into my own hands and started one of those crazy ideas.

"At the time, I just thought they [the banks] thought I wasn't good enough for whatever job it was. Now I realize that they probably knew more about me than I did about myself."

That first crazy idea was VCC Advertising, "my first 'real' business," as Lee puts it. In a nutshell, VCC Advertising put little laminate billboards on the plastic boxes that video rentals come in. Lee and his colleagues networked with 500 video stores around New York, but "the business did not do too well," he says. "Blockbuster came in after a couple of years and killed the little independent video stores with which we partnered."

Then came business school and a short stint as a management consultant at Bain & Company, after which Lee got the entrepreneurial bug again. "I guess you never lose it," he says. A friend of his had access to some advanced supercomputing technology at MIT Lincoln Laboratory at the time, and they were able to license it and start a visual effects tools company called Integrated Computing Engines (ICE). ICE became a key manufacturer of high-performance hardware and software products for the high-resolution computer graphics industry. Lee ran the company for a few years, during its research and development stages, and then handed it off to seasoned professionals managers so he would be free to start GiftCertificates.com.

The original idea for GiftCertificates.com was actually formulated back in 1992, when Lee was in business school. For a class project, he wrote a business plan for a centralized gift certificate clearinghouse. "It took me four years to get around to starting it," he explains, "but that's because I thought that technology was the place to be, and the original incarnation of the company was as an 800-number telephone-based business. I finally got up the nerve to jump off the technology ship and started what was then called 1-800-PRESENT," he says. But by 1998, "it was clear to both me and most of the civilized world . . . that there were tremendous opportunities for business based around the Internet. . . . Funny how things change . . . within a little over a year, we completely shifted from a telephone-based business to an Internet-based business [and came] full circle back to technology."

The idea for GiftCertificates.com was a direct result of having to buy a gift certificate for his sister. "It was a pain in the neck having to go to the department store, wait on two lines, look for a greeting card, try to find a nice box, and then schlep to the post office to wait on line again," he says. "Why not have a central service that did it all for you? It seemed obvious then and now," he adds. "I can't tell you how many people have done the head-knocking gesture and said 'Duh, why didn't I think of that?' when they're told about the company."

A number of other factors motivated Lee to start the business. First, there was the opportunity to build something successful, lasting, and well known. "It's an ego thing," he explains. The second was the opportunity to make money. The third? "What else would I do?" he says. "It sounds corny, but it is in my blood. I don't know how to do anything else. . . . This is what I was born to be—an entrepreneur in a young business that is pioneering a new idea. I would not be happy doing anything else."

### GiftCertificates.com's Key Success Factors

- First-mover advantage
- A large network of business partnerships
- Scale economies
- Know-how in its systems
- Customer service that emphasizes human contact behind Web transactions
- Well-known brand

## PLANS FOR THE FUTURE

The company's biggest risk at this point is operational. "We have invested a large amount of time, expertise, and money to make sure that we can handle the tremendous volume spikes in our business," Lee says. "But if there is any risk, it is that we have underestimated demand." At the same time, GiftCertificates.com is currently expanding its offerings to further meet the unique gift-giving and incentive program needs of corporations and professional service organizations.

Another major growth thrust planned in the next few years includes targeting international business. Because there are so many major markets for GiftCertificates.com outside the United States, particularly in Europe and Asia, the company plans to grow exponentially over the next few years. In fact, the U.S. is only about 30 percent of its target market. "We are lucky that the rest of the world is a year or two behind the U.S. in e-tailing," says Lee. "We have tremendous challenges in getting up to speed just in the U.S. I'm glad the rest of the world is behind. It gives us time to do it right here and to roll it out later elsewhere." As a practical matter, the company plans to market in one country at a time. Sometime in the year 2000, it plans to enter one or two additional developed countries, which it identifies as countries that are about a year or two behind the U.S. in Internet and credit card penetration. "Each [new country we market into] needs to be approached with great care and with the right management team," says Lee.

Like all other venture-backed Internet companies, GiftCertificates.com has an idea of its ultimate goal (i.e.,

its exit strategy) but is not locked into a specific plan.
There could be an IPO if the markets are strong; an acquisition could happen if the right offer comes along; or it
may continue as a private company if that ends up being
the best way of growing business over the next few years.

## Bottom Line: Is GiftCertificates.com Profitable Yet?

GiftCertificates.com evaluates the success of its business
by sales and the total number of active customers acquired.
It does not expect to be profitable for another two to three
years. It is currently in customer acquisition mode. Thus
sales are important for obvious reasons, and the number of
active customer accounts tells the company how effective
it is being at recruiting individual customers, and at what
cost. Lee explains, "E-tailers are generally well schooled in
the economics of lifetime customer value. The simple version is that a customer is thought of as a series of future
cash flows as he or she makes purchases over time. Dis-
counting these cash flows to today, just like a security, gives
you a present value. As long as your cost of acquisition
of customers is below lifetime value, you should invest in
acquisition all day long. You may lose money up-front, but
you make it up later as they keep coming back for additional
purchases." This is why companies such as Amazon.com
support continued losses. As it moves out of acquisition
mode into retention and cross-selling mode, GiftCertifi-
cates.com hopes to move into profitability.

Because GiftCertificates.com was the first mover in the
consumer gift certificates space online, it is the clear
leader in this business category. Competition is fairly

light right now. Only Sparks.com is well funded, and its main mission is to sell physical greeting cards, providing gift certificates only as an add-on. There are also some corporate suppliers of gift certificates for incentives and promotions that have recently ventured online. Yet Gift Certificates.com's comparative advantage is that it built competitive barriers early on: a large network of business partnerships, scale economies, know-how in its systems, the level of top-tier venture support, and (now) a well-known brand. The company plans to maintain its edge by continuing to invest in and advance the status and extent of these assets. "We are ahead in all these areas," says Lee, "but only for as long as we continue to run as fast, or faster, than our future competition."

## Approach to Personnel Management

An important incentive for employees is stock ownership, though stock options are "only a part of winning a person's heart and mind." The company is relaxed about dress code and other minor rules and regulations. It also recognizes a job that is well done and the "raw effort that people put into their work." CEO Lee believes in his role in setting an example. Working hard himself motivates those around him to work hard as well.

## FINDING THE STARRING CAST

For the first two years, GiftCertificates.com was only four people. The company spent a long time simply figuring out its business model and trying to manage outsourced customer service and fulfillment. "It was often pretty bleak back then," says Lee. When the company realized that it needed to shift to a completely Internet-based business, it realized as well that it had to do it right. GiftCertificates.com needed an in-house fulfillment and customer service center, as well as a strong team of technically skilled professionals, designers, marketers, and a lot of cash for brand building," says Lee.

In January 1999, the company embarked on a hiring binge, bringing on senior management with consumer and Internet experience. GiftCertificates.com's management team is largely made up of friends of Lee from high school, business school, and previous jobs. A headhunter also found two key people for the company. Senior management, in turn, brought on directors and managers that they knew.

To start, Lee was lucky enough to secure Richard Marcus as the chairman of his company's board and, through him, connections with significant technology and merchant companies. Marcus was CEO of Neiman Marcus from 1979 to 1988 and an early proponent of technology as a strategic asset. He left Neiman Marcus to pursue ventures at several technology companies, including XcelleNet, Focus Networks, and OnRamp Technologies. Today, Marcus is a senior advisor to Peter J. Solomon Company, the New York City–based investment banking firm and serves on the board of directors of such leading merchant chains as Zale Corporation, Michaels Stores, Waterworks, Inc., and Fashionmall.com.

In addition, GiftCertificates.com has a team of exceptionally qualified senior management. In many cases, Lee sought out his team specifically and pitched his ideas directly to them. Leland Harden, executive vice president of business development and strategy, is a recognized authority on Internet audience development. Before joining GiftCertificates.com, executive vice president of corporate, Max Bardon, headed marketing at Telesensory Corporation, a $40 million consumer technology company, where he built the firm's consumer marketing organization, was architect of its direct marketing programs, and organized its product management and business development functions. Finally, executive vice president of marketing, Bertina Ceccarelli, was formerly the vice president of brand development and research for Snap, where she built the Snap brand and led all NBC-delivered promotional efforts and on-air brand campaigns.

By August, the GiftCertificates.com staff had grown to about sixty people, and by the end of the year, over 100 people. To accommodate its growing staff, the company has a 13,000-square-foot space on two floors in a downtown Manhattan office building. One floor houses the finance, marketing, design, and business development groups. On the other floor are the fulfillment, technology, and customer service groups. Most of the operation, except for fulfillment, resembles any other office. Fulfillment has a factorylike atmosphere because of the big loading area, secure safe room, and massive conveyor belts running all over the place.

## Keeping the Cast Happy

Lee says it is extremely difficult to find the right talent for an Internet start-up "even if you have a great idea, a great team, and substantial financing. Since most companies rarely have all three, it is very hard," he says. "One of the main jobs of a CEO is to recruit talented individuals to join the team."

And how does a company keep talent on board after finding it? Like many other companies, GiftCertificates. com has found that an important incentive for employees is stock ownership. "Sharing a piece of the company with everyone is important because it provides the folks who are financially minded with the brass ring they need to remain motivated," Lee asserts. "It's also important as a symbol that we are all in this together."

Stock options are "only a part of winning a person's heart and mind," he adds. "The most important thing is to recognize a job that is well done, as well as the raw effort that people put into their work."

Lee also finds that working hard himself motivates those who report to him to work hard, which in turn motivates their direct reports to work hard as well. "Just being accessible and walking around helps," he says. "They know I care."

Part of being a growing Internet company is dealing with a crazy business day. GiftCertificates.com employees are intense about getting the job done, but the company is relaxed about dress code and other minor rules and regulations "that can drive some people crazy in the corporate world," says Lee.

He tries to keep everyone focused on whatever the current goal is. The holiday season is obviously a critical period. "Time is our real competition," Lee admits. "We have countdown clocks to Christmas all over the place. I think that it is good that we are in such a seasonal business. Deadlines drive the completion of tasks. We are lucky. Each holiday is a nonartificial, immovable deadline. It makes us a bit nervous and anxious, but that's a good thing."

As for his personal work schedule, Lee walks to work at around 8:30 A.M. each morning. He checks e-mail for an hour and then monitors order flow. Next, he reads feedback to customer service to see if customers are having any problems. Then he checks on the development of a few key items on his personal agenda. Other things he does during each day: "Check on the quality of packages going out the door. Firefight. Meet with my direct reports, a vendor, investors, or a business partner. Review marketing work and advertising. Read industry periodicals. Think." Then he walks home around 11 P.M.

## Advice to Other Internet Entrepreneurs

○ Perform a frank self-assessment and make sure that starting a company is what you want to do.
○ Work very hard to truly understand your market and develop a detailed implementation plan before attempting to obtain financing. The evangelism of an entrepreneur is most important in attracting capital and human resources.
○ Persevere and be ready to bulldoze ahead and keep going no matter what. Never quit when you still have any option to continue.
○ Have good time management.
○ When hiring, "don't trade experience for talent."
○ Be prepared for the time when the business doesn't need you anymore. "At around thirty employees, you as the entrepreneur start to lose the ability to manage every detail. Around sixty people, you need to be noncritical—if a bus hits you, the business needs to continue."

## Securing the Bankroll

A final component of growth (both its impetus and by-product) is the necessity for financing. "It never has been and never will be easy to get someone to part with millions of dollars," he says. "There may be more capital than ever designated for investing in Internet companies, but there are also more ideas and more entrepreneurs than ever.

"And the level of entrepreneurial talent has skyrocketed. It used to be that the best and brightest became doctors, lawyers, investment bankers, or management consultants. Now, you find the top college graduates going right into a start-up. Even CEOs of Fortune 500 companies are getting in on it," he notes.

This meant that GiftCertificates.com had to work very hard to truly understand its market and to develop a detailed implementation plan before it could obtain financing. However, once the company completed its first fund-raising round, it was surprisingly easy to get additional capital.

In November 1999, the company received $18.5 million in new capital from a group of investors co-led by SCP Private Equity Partners, LP (SCP), a private equity investment firm, and Gotham Partners, a New York–based private investment partnership. This round also included the Trump Group of Williams Island, Florida, a prior investor in GiftCertificates.com. This means that the company has raised in excess of $24 million. They have since filed for IPO.

## Getting the Word Out

To take advantage of this cash flow during the 1999 holiday season, GiftCertificates.com allied itself with Grey

Advertising and USWeb/CKS to drive its marketing campaigns, spending $12 million in online and offline advertising in the year's fourth quarter. Consequently, the company's revenue grew from about $2,000 in Web revenue for all of January 1999 to about $500,000 per day by the end of the year. In addition, over 100 leading brand name retailers and over 100 top-name restaurants entrusted their brands to GiftCertificates.com (many on an exclusive basis) in order to acquire existing and emerging online customers.

## ADVICE FROM THE FRONT LINE

In Lee's opinion, anyone who wants to start his or her own business needs to look for "the pain." If you "can develop a solution to something that pains you, chances are there are a lot of other people out there who would pay you for that solution," he says.

He also advises making sure that starting a company is something you really want. "Make sure that you and your family are prepared to make big sacrifices," he says. "Perform a frank self-assessment: Are you the type that thinks you can solve any problem? Have you ever demonstrated excellence in any endeavor before? If you can't answer yes to both of those questions, you probably should not attempt an Internet start-up."

If you do decide to start a business, he thinks the best thing to do is to follow the classic advice of John Paul Getty: "Work hard, strike oil." "Everyone needs a little luck to make it big," says Lee, "but if you aren't prepared to work hard, then when the luck does come around, you'll blow the opportunity."

He also says that persistence pays: "I don't know any

successful entrepreneur who did not have to persevere through difficult times. You have to be a bit pigheaded. It is unreasonable to start a new business. By all thoughtful analysis, every business should fail. There is always competition, and if there isn't, then there is no market. Something critical is always missing; otherwise you'd already have a successful company. But what successful entrepreneurs have in common is the ability to bulldoze ahead and keep going no matter what. Eventually something has to give. Either you become successful or you are put out of business. But the key is not to put yourself out of business. Never quit when you still have any option to continue."

In line with this kind of thinking, Lee holds that the most important resource a seed-stage company has is belief. You need some credibility behind it, he says, but what attracts capital and human resources the most is the evangelism of an entrepreneur.

The people you hire and the quality of your advisors are also crucial. When hiring employees, "don't trade experience for talent," says Lee. It's also important for a start-up CEO to have a few people he or she respects and can pick up the phone and call at any time, whether about a business issue or simply for moral support. In Lee's case, he has his chairman, Richard Marcus, a well-respected retailer who "has seen many more wars." Lee also has a couple of friends who are successful entrepreneurs and make good sounding boards for his problems. He believes that having those kinds of resources is more important than a formal advisory board.

Having good staff members and advisors also takes some of the load off the CEO's shoulders, although "it is important to realize that your work will never be finished," says Lee. "There is always something more that needs to get done." Consequently, he thinks that time management, a result of how you prioritize your day, is vital. And, of course, some of being productive on a highly compressed time frame is simply becoming accustomed to it. "I have been asked many times how I handle the stress of so many things going on at one time," says Lee. "I think that I have just gotten used to it. It's what I expect, so it's normal."

He also says that hiring a competent personal assistant, someone who is tuned in to what's going on with him, was undoubtedly one of the best things that he's ever done, and it's allowed him to be about 30 percent more productive. "And since she's smart, I don't have to double-check everything," he says. "In fact, she double-checks on me!" In addition, he finds that as a CEO, "it is okay to be a bit rude" and cut meetings down to the barebone essentials. By forcing an agenda, he can usually cut meeting times down by 25 percent.

Also important is keeping up with changing technologies. Lee reads every issue of industry periodicals such as *The Red Herring, The Industry Standard, Business 2.0,* and *FastCompany*. By the time he has finished reading an issue, he has five or so pages ripped out with some sort of action item scribbled on them.

Finally, Lee advises emphasizing customer service and making sure there is human contact behind Web transactions. "The customer service department is the front line of the business. If our customers have a problem, they let us know it," he says. As CEO, Lee actually has all customer service e-mail forwarded to him in real-time and spends about an hour a day scanning the messages to see whether customers are having problems with the site, are confused about any promotion the company might be running, or don't understand what services it offers. He also talks at least twice a day with the company's customer service representatives to see if there are any unusual trends developing. GiftCertificates.com also provides a phone number (1-800-PRESENT) for Internet customers to call if they have questions or difficulties. "Knowing you can reach out and touch someone helps build trust," Lee says.

The company doesn't do focus groups because they are too expensive and too prone to bias based on a single, strongly opinionated individual. Instead, it does what it calls user studies. The Web site asks customers to do specific things and then watches what happens. Can they find the button? Do they get confused by the font? Do they give up and leave the site to start surfing? That, GiftCertificates.com finds, is the most helpful kind of information.

"And remember," Lee says, "just because you are an online business doesn't mean you don't have a storefront. You do, it's just not a physical one. Instead, your home page is your storefront. For customers to keep coming back, it needs to be kept fresh, inviting, exciting, and simple to understand, just like a real storefront."

### Vision of the New Economy

Over the next five years, as Internet usage expands internationally and across age groups, this increase in scale will allow companies to reach niche markets in a much more cost-effective manner. Also within five years, look for the evolution of immersive, interactive, microtargeted online advertising that actually works.

## The Power of the Internet

When asked what its business can do through the Internet that it couldn't do through traditional means, Gift Certificates.com responds with the following list:

- Give more information to help customers make decisions
- Provide greater selection
- Reduce costs
- Enhance quality control
- Take advantage of many business partnerships and revenue-sharing opportunities
- Attract better people and more capital
- Efficiently remarket to an existing base of customers

Clearly, the company is a believer in the power of the Web. Lee says that other advantages of being an Internet-based company are that "you can write the rules and see the effect of their implementation" and perhaps bear "the financial fruits of being a successful innovator."

He adds, "Internet companies are for people who want to be part of something new and are willing to work hard to make it happen. If you gravitate toward that type of environment, it's the ideal place to work. If you don't, it will seem like the company wants too much from you. It is not for people who believe one should work to live, not live to work."

Working for an Internet company is also different from a traditional business because of speed, Lee says. "Everything happens faster. Time to market for new products is increased. Competition is faster and smarter."

There are "few rules, and energy often conquers all, but lots of mistakes."

He also thinks that working for an Internet company has changed over the past year. "It has become more of a game for professionals," he says. "It is difficult for companies to come out of dorm rooms or garages anymore." This is because many of the ventures getting funded these days have senior management teams from Fortune 500 companies or are founded by entrepreneurs on their second or third Internet venture. "It used to be that nobody really knew what they were doing, so anyone could play the game," he explains. "Today, the bar has been raised."

Companies Lee and his colleagues particularly admire include Amazon.com and eToys.com because they do an excellent job of anticipating the consumer's needs. "That means keeping pages simple and designing with the customer's fears and expectations in mind," Lee says. "It's one of the hardest things to do. Web designers are, by definition, Web savvy. But you have to design for the nonsavvy customer."

Despite his admiration for these companies, if Lee were given the choice to run any other Internet company that currently exists, he would pick Microsoft Corp. "They have a pretty good thing going," he says. "As CEO, the raw power that courses through your veins each morning must be quite a kick."

Interestingly, Lee does very little online shopping himself. "I like to go to shops and buy stuff that I can touch. . . . I even buy my computers in a store," he admits. He mostly uses the Internet to check e-mail and perform research on other e-tailers.

Even so, Lee has some strong opinions on how the Internet is changing the landscape of business and creating new opportunities. While there may be some companies that are overhyped right now, he believes the general excitement about the Internet is valid, "and it is just picking up steam," he says. "The thing about the Internet is that its growth fuels further growth. As the audience becomes bigger, more businesses make sense that did not before." As a result, new businesses come into existence in order to provide newly needed services to newly created companies. Thus, "we truly are seeing only the tip of the iceberg," Lee says.

In his mind, the change in the Internet over the next few years will primarily be one of scale. While there is currently a privileged class of Internet users who "get it," they are mostly in the United States and are neither very old nor very young. This group will broaden over the next five years as Internet usage expands internationally and across age groups. According to Lee, this increase in scale will allow companies to reach niche markets in a much more cost-effective manner. The addressable market for certain niches will expand dramatically, and new Internet companies will emerge to capitalize on them.

One area that he thinks has the potential to be particularly profitable in the near future: anything that can make advertising more efficient. In his opinion, offline advertising efforts frequently do not produce results. "Think about how much advertising gets wasted on you each day," he says. "Someone's paying for it. If that business can be made more rational and efficient, both the advertisers and [their audiences] would be much happier."

Hopefully, the move away from basing advertising rates on CPMs (clicks per thousand) and toward more variable advertising models online will help force this kind of rationalization. Since you can directly measure the performance of an Internet ad, Lee says, a marketer can direct advertising to companies that perform well and away from those that do not: "It's Direct Marketing 101." In the world of direct mail, you measure the performance of lists and creatives. The ones that work, you do more of. The ones that don't, you avoid. The same thing will be true on the Internet."

In the world of online advertising, he explains, each impression, click-through, and buy-through can be tracked. If you as an advertiser know how much you paid for an ad, you can calculate your return on investment. Therefore, online advertising will more likely be held to a higher standard than offline advertising; the precise measurement available to geotarget will force it to evolve quickly. Internet technologies and the massive number of "microaudiences" the Web has created allow marketers to home in on very specific demographics. Advertising providers use this ability to increase the effectiveness of their ads, something we are already seeing with ad-serving networks such as DoubleClick. Ad-serving networks use technology to target ads to specific types of people.

However, microtargeting will not be enough, according to Lee. "True mesmerizing, brand-building, kick-ass advertising that really sells will not happen on the Web until broadband arrives," he says. "In five years, I hope to see the evolution of immersive, interactive, microtargeted online advertising that actually works."

But overall, Lee thinks the best thing that could happen to the Internet industry, at least in terms of the effect on his own business, would be a 2000 holiday season that records three times the sales of 1999 and outstrips most projections. He says the worst thing that could happen would be for customers to get spooked by a big privacy or security blowup at a major site such as Amazon.com, and then for the media to blow it out of proportion. "But even an event like that would heal over time," he says.

In the end, Lee loves working for a company that takes advantage of the immense capabilities of the Internet and allows his entrepreneurial spirit to thrive. "The most rewarding aspect is building a business that doesn't need you," he says. "In the beginning, it's all you. You write the business plan, take out the trash [such as business plan drafts], and manage the books. But at a certain point, around thirty people, you start to lose the ability to manage every detail. Around sixty people, you need to be noncritical—not unneeded, but if a bus hits you, the business needs to continue. For me, getting a company to that stage is extremely rewarding. It's akin to creating a lasting work of art."

For Lee, it's extremely rewarding to see "a great idea get implemented well and customers actually positively responding. I suppose for any entrepreneur, seeing the business actually work is truly a dream come true."

# 8

# eTradersEdge.com

*An inside look at the attempt of eTradersEdge.com to capitalize on the rapidly changing and highly lucrative online financial services industry*

Because Internet-based trading systems have an immediate global footprint, there's a lot of pressure to trade all the time, forgetting time zones and daytime hours, receiving foreign exchange and other international data. Anticipating the next steps in online trading, eTradersEdge.com provides online investors and online investing firms with content and strategies about the next generation of investing and order-matching technology, ECNs (electronic communication networks). ECN technology supports electronic direct access trading (E-DAT), which creates mini stock exchanges that allow you to directly trade with another individual and eliminate the middleman.

eTradersEdge.com gives online investors a wealth of information on topics related to online trading, including after-hours trading, ECNs, and day trading, as well as details on what specific online brokers are offering for active and advanced online investors. It offers educational tools for all levels of investors and forums for users to discuss how to capitalize on the new technologies. The company also provides strategic consulting services and creates custom content for online brokers looking to educate their users on the capabilities of electronic trading.

Online brokerages are fueling the growing volume of trading activity, so much so that billion-share trading days are becoming the norm. For example, Charles Schwab alone gets 100,000 new online accounts monthly. By some estimates, by 2002, nearly 14 million stock trade accounts will be set up through online brokerage firms. The key for these online brokers will be their ability to create an easy-to-use interface and enough educational material to help their customers feel comfortable taking advantage of that interface. All these accounts will be potential consumers of value-added financial content such as eTradersEdge.com offers.

## Fast-Track Facts

| | |
|---|---|
| **Key Executive** | Jon Edwards, CEO |
| **Business Model** | Value-added financial content and services provider; revenue comes from consulting and sponsorship deals with customers |
| **Target Customers** | Online investing firms and individual online investors |

## The Genesis of an Idea

For a long time, Wall Street professionals were the only ones who had the tools necessary to access the financial markets directly. Everyone else had to use a third-party (a broker) to place trades. Gradually, over the past ten years, the rules have begun to change, giving individual investors greater access to the markets. In 1997, NASDAQ added ECNs to its automated quotations system, making quotes and order sizes finally available to individual investors. Simply put, this meant that for the first time individual investors would be able to get the information they needed to trade directly with the Wall Street professionals. These technological developments are forcing the New York Stock Exchange to make changes that would have been unimaginable only a few years ago.

Realizing that the world's financial markets are undergoing significant change, almost all top online brokerage firms are now scrambling to form relationships with ECNs so that they can offer some level of direct access and after-hours trading to their customers. The founders and employees of eTradersEdge.com believe ECNs are merely the first step in eliminating traditional middlemen. They envision a future when global financial markets will be open to all investors all of the time.

Banking on the assumption that everyone who wants to trade will eventually use electronic trading to access the markets in some way, the company's founders started their business. Two facts in particular inspired them: the incredible rate at which investing technology is advancing, and the lack of information available to explain its functionality to the intended users. Because market ac-

cess is now so different from the way it has been conducted over the past twenty years and will only continue
to change, it is important to provide information and educational tools that customers can easily digest. The company therefore jumped on the excellent opportunity to
provide valuable information to both online investors
and online investing firms.

Hopefully, eTradersEdge.com will be just the starting point. The company is also coming out with a series
of books about how online investors can make the jump
to E-DAT. As a believer in creating a presence in as many
media as possible, eTradersEdge.com is exploring options
such as hosting education-oriented events through Web-
casts and traditional media outlets, as well as creating
customized educational tools to be hosted directly on the
sites of client-company online investing firms.

One of the most unusual aspects of eTradersEdge.com
is its news team dedicated to the new technology available to online investors. Team members have extensive
experience as online investors and electronic traders, and
they share their understanding of the technology behind
the new trading techniques in an easy-to-understand
format and language. Because the technology is so new
and is, for now, much more complicated than just entering the number of shares you want and pressing Enter,
it will be crucial for online investing firms to create an
easy-to-use interface for their members to access this
technology. eTradersEdge.com plans to position itself as
the vendor of choice for helping online brokers make
their systems user-friendly and creating customized educational content for them to provide to their online
investors.

## A Brief Overview of ECNs

1. There are about fifteen main ECNs, although only about eight are live systems at present. They include Island (owned by Datek Online), ATTAIN (All-Tech), Bloomberg Tradebook (Bloomberg), and Instinet (Reuters). Most ECNs are usually owned by, or somehow associated with, online brokerage firms.

2. The ECN matches up buyers and sellers, usually of NASDAQ stocks. These traders are usually the brokerage firm's own customers. The ECN takes trading volume off the exchange floors (i.e., the established exchanges, such as NYSE or AMEX). With an ECN, a brokerage can quickly match a trade in its own book and execute the trade, potentially bypassing the NASDAQ system.

3. At present, a best bid or offer from an ECN must be reported into the NASDAQ trading system. ECNs work with the major exchanges and are licensed. However, a Securities and Exchange Commission (SEC) ruling, which establishes alternative exchanges, makes it unclear whether ECNs will in the future maintain these associations with the major exchanges or become independent exchanges in their own right.

Because this new trading model is only beginning to emerge, online investing firms that do not provide information about the new technologies and methods will be passed over in favor of the ones that do. "What online investors and online investor firms will find most useful about eTradersEdge.com," says CEO Jon Edwards, "is our ability to provide easy-to-understand content about such a complicated technology. In addition, we are able to tap into the desires of current online investors from our Web site to find out what they find to be the most useful sources of information. It is a win-win situation for everyone—that is, except for professional Wall Street traders who are seeing their closely guarded secrets escape into public domain."

In sum, the goal for eTradersEdge.com is to empower as many people as possible with the best knowledge possible to capitalize on new investing technology. The financial services marketplace is clearly one of the key sectors in the Internet, and online investing is one of the most empowering tools to come out of the Internet revolution. As technology continues to advance, it will be a race to see who can provide the best and easiest-to-use tools for online investors to capitalize on electronic direct access to the markets.

## eTradersEdge.com's Key Success Factors

- Establishing a news team dedicated to the new technology available to online investors
- Finding capital and understanding what benefits a capital source can bring to the table, other than sorely needed cash
- Forming an advisory board based on more than members' pedigrees, such as their willingness to help the company
- Hiring the right people
- Developing the right strategic partnerships that validate your business model
- Providing a value-added product or service that keeps improving
- Creating natural barriers to entry in your field that will protect you from competitors of all sizes

## The Magic of the Internet

eTradersEdge.com was founded on the belief that the Internet is fundamentally changing every industry, but the financial services industry especially. The remarkable part is that there is no real tangible aspect to the Internet; it simply makes the transfer of information much more efficient. As Edwards says, "Almost every established company now uses the Internet in some way or another to augment their business. Some only use it for marketing purposes while others use it as their primary marketplace. Can you believe that maybe only one percent of companies had a Web site five years ago? Imagine the amount of business created from just helping these businesses establish Web sites. This does not even count the more complex functions that most Web sites now incorporate."

Edwards also says that "people incorrectly assume that all the good Internet businesses have been taken. They think the stock market is going to crash soon and that the Internet has reached its peak. No way. Every company must incorporate the Internet into its strategy somehow or it will become extinct soon, no matter how large it is."

The Internet is what has made direct access to financial markets possible. New companies are making an entire business out of developing Internet-based software that allows direct access to the markets through ECNs, and most ECNs are now partnering with online brokerage firms to capitalize on these new investors.

As people become comfortable with online investing very quickly, E-DAT is the next logical step. The Internet has created an environment in which, soon, it will not just be for advanced and active traders but everyone. After-hours trading is already offered by E\*TRADE, DLJdirect, Schwab, Datek, and other online brokers.

"As the world's financial markets continue to undergo radical change, most online investors still have no idea of the capabilities that are evolving from it," explains Edwards. "They are still getting their first taste of IPOs and the ability to access a wealth of new information online. . . . Online brokers, however, are smart and are starting to form relationships that will enable them to offer direct access as well; you will still have to pay similar fees, but you will be trading directly."

These aren't the only reasons Edwards loves the Internet. "I am an avid Internet user," he says. "I am online probably eight to ten hours a day at work and then on for another hour or so at home. It is hard to believe I ever lived without it. The Internet provides you with access to so much information. Being a highly motivated person, it empowers me to just keep learning about new things. The information is just there waiting for the taking."

And working at an Internet company is different from working at other companies, he says. "The environment of an Internet company tends to be alive, and not just because music is playing and people are running around at a frantic pace. There is much more a sense of community because the people working there are usually owners in the company as well. Having a potential big pot of gold at the end of the rainbow is a great incentive. Also, the environment of Internet companies tends to be much more casual, which makes it much more fun to come to work."

His advice to others in the Internet world is to always keep your eyes open to the many great business opportunities the Internet offers. "CEOs should always be looking to engage in other businesses, whether as investors or simply brainstorming for new ideas to develop. We tend to get so caught up and busy with what we are doing that it can be difficult to take a step back and notice the other opportunities. Sometimes these other opportunities can end up being more successful than your current venture."

If he could do anything in the world other than what he's doing right now, Edwards would travel the world starting new ventures. "There is an unbelievable thrill that comes with being a part of any start-up," he says. "Because everyone is forced to wear so many hats, it creates a better team atmosphere and makes for an incredible work environment. There are so many untapped niches out there just waiting to be taken advantage of— and there is nothing I would rather do than take advantage of all of them. In addition, I am a strong believer that even existing businesses should be looking to start additional ventures, at every stage. They often have the best resources, both financially and in terms of human resources, to capitalize on new opportunities.

Yet "so many big companies just sat back and let all these start-ups develop new companies and steal their market share away and exploit new markets," he continues. "It took an incredibly long time for them to wake up [to the Internet] and start capitalizing on it as well—and in many cases it was too late. Do you think that Toys 'R' Us or Barnes & Noble will ever be the same now that eToys and Amazon.com have entered the marketplace? Innovation, speed, and creativity wins, regardless of how big you are or how much money you have."

## INSIDER TIPS

In its short existence, eTradersEdge.com has already learned many lessons about the best way to forge a new business. "Although our founders have had experience starting businesses in the past, each new venture is entirely different. It's like playing cards; [in each round] you are dealt a new hand," says Edwards.

For all Internet start-ups, three of the keys to success are finding capital, forming an advisory board, and hiring the right people. These factors are what jump-start a company.

Edwards has found that obtaining capital is often easiest when you need it the least. This usually means that your company is doing something right, so others want to get in on the action. eTradersEdge.com's advice is to follow the old adage, "Only take on capital when you need it." However, it can make sense to take on capital when the person or entity providing the capital is also providing intangible assets, like great connections. Venture capital firms are known for forming *keiretsus*, or networks of companies, around the companies they have funded, and this is always a big advantage. Understanding what benefits a capital source can bring to the table, other than sorely needed cash, is also extremely important. "The key is developing a realistic business model from the start that can generate enough cash to grow the business in the short run and provide the opportunity to make big bucks in the long run," says Edwards.

eTradersEdge.com also subscribes to the theory that a good advisory board is absolutely critical to any start-up company. Advisers should be individuals who have extensive experience in your industry and, more important, a desire to assist your business. Businesses often pick poor advisory boards because they are more interested in members' pedigrees rather than in their willingness to help the company. Each member of the board, as well as every employee, no matter his or her position in the company, needs to be ambitious and have a desire to impact the business. This is because everyone involved with a start-up company has the ability to significantly affect its success, regardless of the company's size or the level of the employee.

As mentioned many times in this book already, finding the right talent for an Internet company can be extremely difficult. There are so many opportunities available to qualified employees that it's important to create incentives for people to come and work with you. eTradersEdge.com offers a stock option plan that allows employees to become part owners and encourages them to be consistently thinking outside the box in terms of new ideas for the company.

"We encourage our employees to brainstorm on what they are doing and what the company as a whole could be doing at least once a month," explains Edwards. "Fresh ideas are the lifeblood of every business, and they should not just be encouraged in upper management." eTradersEdge.com even encourages employees to brainstorm for ideas about new ventures. "Most people do not realize the degree to which they can leverage each step the business takes into even greater things," Edwards says. Whether it is an innovative idea that develops from your current business or a new technology you create, the opportunities are endless. One door open leads to a whole new set of doors that can be opened.

"The most challenging part is that there are so many opportunities and only twenty-four hours in every day," he adds. "There are so many incredible opportunities, and ideas that I have personally, that I would love nothing more than to have a couple hundred million dollars to go build a couple of different companies simultaneously."

Especially helpful in this process of brainstorming is to bounce ideas off talented friends and business associates. It is a good idea to sit down and simply write out all of the people you know. Then, list what they do and whom they know. "You will be amazed how many resources this simple exercise will provide and doors it will open," Edwards says, although he cautions that "you do have to open the doors yourself. Regardless of how good of contacts you may think you have, very rarely will they just magically turn into business. Getting in the door is just the first step. You still have to close the deal."

Another key to running a successful Internet company is keeping on top of constantly changing technology. Edwards tries to read prominent Internet and business publications, such as *The Red Herring, The Industry Standard, Wired, Silicon Alley Reporter, BusinessWeek,* and *FastCompany,* to keep abreast of what new companies are getting funded. "The more you read, the more you know," he says, "especially in an industry that changes so quickly." He finds that *The Industry Standard* is usually a reliable barometer of what new technologies, products, or services are being developed. This is because, as he says, "Venture capitalists are usually plugged in to what is going on, and when a company gets funded, they are usually onto something."

eTradersEdge.com has also learned that strategic partnerships are extremely important to the life of any Internet company. "Developing the right partnerships almost validates your business model," says Edwards. However, as a smaller business, it's important to make sure that you are not getting the short end of the stick. As with any business arrangement, a good deal is a fair deal. You need to be realistic when approaching larger businesses and present them with a clear-cut plan that benefits both sides. Since eTradersEdge.com is one of the first content and strategic advisory companies to emerge from the electronic trading field, it is being selective about its partnerships. Yet because it plans to attract users to its own site through valuable information and special deals, as well as provide content to other sites, the pursuit of strategic partnerships is particularly important. "It is much easier to live one click down in the Internet world and gradually build traffic from a number of different sources," says Edwards.

The Internet is a great equalizer. The key to being a successful company, in any industry or of any size, is providing a value-added product or service that keeps improving. There are so many different niches to fill that it would be impossible for any one company to occupy all of them. There will always be competitors and people trying to copy your idea. You just have to try to stay one step ahead of them. This means continually improving your customer's experience and adding new components. "In addition, once you have customers, they are yours to lose," says Edwards. "Over time, if you keep excelling in each of these areas, you will be able to create natural barriers to entry that will protect you from competitors of all sizes."

Finally, eTradersEdge.com recommends that anyone starting an Internet business diversify. Starting an Internet business can be risky (as can anything), but if you diversify yourself by trying a couple of different strategies or ideas, your chance for success is that much greater. This doesn't mean that throwing yourself entirely into one business concept is a bad idea; just leave enough room within your business model to take it a couple of different ways. "[To] go where the paying clients are is always a good rule of thumb," says Edwards." And give yourself some time to get going; don't expect success overnight. It definitely takes time. You have to prove yourself."

## Advice to Other Internet Entrepreneurs

- Follow the old adage, "Only take on capital when you need it."
- Diversify yourself by trying a couple of different strategies and your chance for success is that much greater. "Go where the paying clients are" is always a good rule of thumb.
- Seek customer feedback.
- Learn to manage your time; one of the most important characteristics of a successful entrepreneur is the ability to adapt to change—and quickly.
- Remember, there is always a solution to every obstacle.

## METRICS OF SUCCESS

Profitability is the most obvious measure of a company's success. Because the Internet itself is in such an early stage of its growth, many Internet companies are more concerned with attracting users and eyeballs than with the financial bottom line right now. eTradersEdge.com thinks profitability should be just as important for an Internet company as it is for any other company. It will be interesting to see who can turn eyeballs into profits. For its part, eTradersEdge.com is extremely focused on providing the most useful experience for online investors, but it sees no reason why it cannot be profitable along the way. Its major source of revenue comes from consulting and sponsorship deals with individual online investing firms. It is currently in talks with a number of different online financial companies about developing educational products designed specifically for their needs.

eTradersEdge.com also evaluates the success of its business by the number of new people it helps become comfortable with new investing technology. The company is highly focused on making its Web site and educational material user-friendly. Providing clear, succinct information that is very distinct from the jargon-laden "trader speak" used by Wall Street professionals is deemed essential for getting all levels of investors comfortable with the technology.

"There is a reason so few people know about what is happening on Wall Street. Knowledge is power, and Wall Street professionals have been trying to keep out the individual investors for as long as possible," says Edwards. For him, the most gratifying aspect of eTradersEdge.com is the feeling of accomplishment he gets from helping people get comfortable with the new technology. "You will find," he says, "that most professional traders cannot 'speak down' to a normal investor's level. Because we have experience on both sides of the fence, we are able to communicate our message in ways for everyone to comprehend."

The company maintains its competitive edge by trying to constantly improve its customers' experiences. It actively seeks customer feedback and offers free information as well as educational content on a subscription basis. eTradersEdge.com also has customers' names, addresses, phone numbers, and e-mail addresses on file so that it can send them its daily update and keep them abreast of new developments in the industry.

To that end, eTradersEdge.com places great importance on customer feedback. It encourages users to post information, ask questions, and tell the company how to give them a better experience through additional products and services that customers would find of interest. This feedback is also helpful for advertisers, who are able to learn specific pieces of information about what they can do to attract customers.

### Approach to Personnel Management

eTradersEdge.com offers a stock option plan that allows employees to become part owners and encourages them to brainstorm and think like business owners. "Fresh ideas are the lifeblood of every business and they should not just be encouraged in upper management," says CEO Jon Edwards.

## THOUGHTS FROM THE TOP

According to Edwards, every day as the CEO of an Internet company is different. Because everything in the Internet world moves at the speed of light, you have to be on your toes. That means reacting to competition, capitalizing on an opportunity when you see it, and creating barriers to entry. No company is safe from competitors anymore. Much of every day is spent planning, trying to create new innovative products and services, examining potential growth areas, and staving off competitors.

Because it can be difficult for CEOs of start-ups to manage their time with so many things going on at once, Edwards suggests setting aside specific time every day to accomplish certain tasks. "With so much happening so quickly, it is extremely easy to be consumed by a million different things at once," he says. There's a fine line to be walked, because one of the most important characteristics of a successful entrepreneur is the ability to adapt to change—and quickly. That means rearranging schedules, forming focus groups, and turning on a dime. The trick is to be able to do these things when necessary but not consistently wonder at the end of the day what you actually completed during your time at work. Everyone needs daily, monthly, and annual goals.

"The most challenging aspect of starting and owning your own business," Edwards asserts, "is that you are responsible for every action the company takes. Especially at the very beginning, when something important needs to get done, you need to do it. There is no one who is going to do it for you or hold your hand along the way. You are the last line of defense. The lessons you learn can only be learned by doing. If you have never started and built a business before, your skills are decidedly undermatched in certain areas against someone who has."

"It is so exciting to have an idea and be able to see it come to fruition," he adds. "That is the best part about starting a business: When you have these ideas, you can run with them. There is nothing holding you back. There will always be obstacles, but you find a way to work around them. That is probably the best thing you learn as an entrepreneur; there is always a solution to every obstacle. Too many people butt their heads up against a wall and never try again. There is always a way to get around it, or through it. You just have to focus on thinking outside the box."

Another challenge, according to Edwards, is that there are so many companies competing for untapped niches in the marketplace. The problem is that so many areas online are already being tapped; it is as if the areas deemed harder to access are the most attractive at this point. For example, selling alcohol over the Internet is not an easy business model, but once someone is able to overcome all of the legal and logistics issues involved, it will be a goldmine. Venture capitalists are so flush with cash right now that there has never been a better time to start an Internet venture, provided you have the right ideas, experience, and connections. What most people still do not realize is that although it seems easy to attract capital right now, only those that have the right industry knowledge are getting it.

Other online businesses that Edwards uses most include information sites, such as Hoovers, which helps him to keep learning about what other companies are doing. Most people incorrectly assume that if a company has already exploited a new idea, there are no other opportunities. By analyzing the new developments of companies, Edwards is able to make his own judgments about the products, services, or technologies they are offering and whether there would be any complementary business opportunities to it.

If he could run any other Internet company that currently exists, he would choose to run Microsoft Corp. "They have their hands in so many different baskets," he says. "Even with the monopoly conviction, [Microsoft] could spur even further domination by forcing greater innovation in different areas. Although most people like to disparage Bill Gates, I give him a world of credit. You know you are a good entrepreneur when the government has to step in and tell you that you have created a monopoly."

Other companies Edwards admires are the ones that are starting to put their money back to work in start-ups. Examples of these are Lycos and Rare Medium. Putting money back into start-ups is an excellent investment and a way to diversify your operations. He also admires idealab! and some of the other incubator companies, because his personality is such that he is most drawn to entrepreneurs and companies that are always looking for new business ventures.

### Vision of the New Economy

The technology behind electronic trading will soon enable anyone to invest in overseas securities. In addition, an enormous number of overseas investors will want to start tapping into U.S. securities. As for the future of the Internet in general, expect to see more companies more actively developing additional businesses in the Internet realm. Too many talented employees are leaving companies to start new ventures that could be harnessed in-house. Big companies will eventually wake up and start tapping into these opportunities. "Some of the most successful companies in the future will end up being holding companies that house a number of ventures in various industries," says Edwards.

His most important piece of advice for people starting their own business is this: "Believe in yourself. There are always going to be individuals who do not agree with your idea and try and cut you down," he says. Look at Dell, for example. "There are also always going to be unpleasant people to deal with. The key is to just keep focused on your vision and not let anyone get you down. This is not to say that you should not be realistic if your idea is not working. You should at the outset make clearly defined goals for your business and realistically judge where your business should be at certain points in the future. However, the key is to believe in yourself. Anything is possible. You just have to find a way to make it work."

## WHAT'S NEXT?

Plans and strategies for eTradersEdge.com change every day. There are so many exciting opportunities for business development that the company is constantly updating and enhancing its strategy. And the more technology advances, the more need there will be for the company's services. Because every single investor will be affected by electronic trading, eTradersEdge.com has a huge market to tap into.

This market potential includes overseas expansion and marketing to a worldwide audience. The site will eventually be available in a number of different languages as well. The financial markets are heading toward one global marketplace that will be open to everyone at all times. Online investing and personal financial services online are just starting to take off overseas, and the technology behind electronic trading will soon enable anyone to invest in overseas securities. In addition, an enormous number of overseas investors will want to start tapping into U.S. securities. Investors worldwide are going to be amazed by the number of investing opportunities they will have available to them—not just how they can invest, but where they can invest. eTradersEdge.com will be there to educate them.

## Bottom Line: Is eTradersEdge.com Profitable Yet?

For now, eTradersEdge.com is focused on building a valuable company and providing the best content possible to its customers. Like almost all entrepreneurs, Edwards is interested in building a company of value, something that will end up making him and his employees a lot of money. Because of the nature of its business, eTradersEdge.com is more likely to be bought than it is to go public. Potential buyers would be a larger consulting firm or an online firm that wants it as its exclusive educational/information arm. The company thinks this will prove to be an effective exit strategy at some point. But you never know.

As for the future of the Internet in general, Edwards believes that twenty years from now, we will be including a whole new group of company names in the class with Coca-Cola, General Motors, and Wal-Mart. "And I don't mean just AOL, Cisco, and Microsoft," says Edwards. "There will be other companies that have not even been started yet, that are just simmering in the minds of entrepreneurs, waiting to be taken advantage of. The fundamental landscape of the world economy is changing."

The only potential downside, he believes, "is if some of the smaller Internet companies that have recently gone public just tank. Too many companies with no earnings or track record are going public. It will be impossible for all of these companies to make it. Too many of them have still not made a nickel in profit. There will continue to be a shakeout, but hopefully it will not disrupt the markets as a whole too much."

Finally, Edwards and his colleagues are also interested in how the Internet will continue to change our lives. The line between computers and PCs is already becoming blurred. TVs are still, on average, much less expensive than PCs, but this will change as broadband technology is rolled out to mass markets. With broadband access catching on quickly, it will only be a matter of time before you are watching "Ally McBeal" on television and clicking on her sweater to buy it, owing to the interactivity of the Internet. According to Edwards, "Anyone who thinks that Internet advertising ends with banner ads is very much in the dark."

Edwards also anticipates a flood of products, services, and technologies evolving from overseas. "Because many countries are just getting going, it is only a matter of time before smart people start figuring out things that we have yet to develop." In addition, eTradersEdge.com expects to see companies taking on a more active role in developing additional businesses. Too many talented employees are leaving companies to start new ventures that could be harnessed in-house. Big companies will eventually wake up and start tapping into these opportunities. "Some of the most successful companies in the future will end up being holding companies that house a number of ventures in various industries," Edwards predicts.

The Internet already affects almost everyone in the world in some way or another, whether or not they realize it. And with still only a fraction of the world owning computers and so many Internet opportunities still untapped, the effects of the Internet are only starting to be felt. "We feel that eTradersEdge.com is well positioned for our segment of the industry. Because so many individuals are already using online investing on some level, the next step for many of these individuals will be to harness the power of electronic direct access to the markets. Many investors are beginning to experiment with after-hours trading, which primarily uses the same technology. The words *ECN* and *market maker* are still foreign to most online investors. In a matter of a few years, we hope to make them common speak and very understandable to every level of online investor."

# 9

# Foofoo.com

*The story of a "chichi" Web site and its attempts to create a name for itself in the world of high society—on the Internet*

Headed by a team of experienced Web entrepreneurs, including president and CEO Connie Ling, Foofoo.com is one of the first companies to target the generation that today is using the Internet for everything from picking the best wines to reading the morning newspaper and investing in the stock market. Foofoo combines content from a wide range of upscale publishing partners (e.g., *Vogue, Men's Health, Elle, Travel & Leisure,* and *Food & Wine*) with high-end, hard-to-find products from commerce partners. Foofoo.com wants to be the definitive authority on the Internet for the fun and finer things in life.

This privately held company—headquartered in Arlington, Virginia, and founded in January 1999—is creating a new model for destination sites online by leveraging well-known brands and aggregating content, commerce, and advertising to attract this largely untapped audience of upwardly mobile individuals online.

## THE BRAINSTORM

By the end of 1998, the founders of Foofoo had been in the Internet field for an average of four years (both on the consulting and sales ends) and had seen a lot of ideas come and go. All were in agreement about one thing: While the Internet provides ample opportunities to do research, much of the content out there is of poor quality and badly organized.

Foofoo's founders believed that while many Web sites are focused on a particular product or product line from a manufacturer, consumers are interested in opinions from many sources: manufacturers, magazine articles, and each other. They thought: Why not be the source of this information for the high-end audience? They felt that the upscale market had been neglected for too long and was a niche waiting to be filled.

### *Fast-Track Facts*

| | |
|---|---|
| *CEO* | Connie Ling |
| *Business Model* | Business-to-consumer e-tailer |
| *Funding* | Private investors |
| *Business Partners* | 500 commerce partners, including Sky Guide, Healing Retreats and Spas, Departures, and American Express; Publishing partners include *Vogue, Men's Health, Elle, Travel & Leisure, Food & Wine* |
| *Target Customers* | Upwardly mobile individuals |

The company's principal founder and chairman had always been in the habit of purchasing the best of everything. His friends' nickname for him was in fact "Foofoo." But as he spent more and more time online, he realized that most of what could be bought on the Internet was of inferior quality. To purchase finer products, such as clothing from luxury designers and unique artifacts, you had to visit shops and boutiques. That's where the idea to start a company that offered the best of everything online came from. And the name "Foofoo" was a natural. It's actually a play on the word *froufrou*, which originated in eighteenth-century France. As well-born ladies made their entrances at parties, the silk of their dresses would make a distinctive "frou-frou" sound. This onomatopoeic usage became synonymous with fancy or high-end items.

Foofoo soon defined its mission as becoming the online authority on "the fun and finer things in life." The idea: cut through all the garbage on the Internet and deliver a useful, engaging experience. "We want to be an oasis of quality and style in a desert of unoriginal and pedestrian e-commerce sites," says Ling. "Is something fun? Is it finer? If so, it just might be Foofoo! That's been our mantra, our litmus test."

Not surprisingly, Foofoo's target customers are upwardly mobile consumers who feel they are technically savvy, time-constrained, and ever eager to know "what's hot." The company's vision also incorporates a belief that people want a Web site that is more than just a place to buy a product. Foofoo offers e-commerce, but it also provides content through articles that give shoppers easy ways to find out which designers are hot, read about an

194

exciting ski adventure, or gather information about luxurious gifts for the opposite sex.

Although providing products is only a small part of its e-commerce package, ordering, fulfillment, delivery, and customer care are nonetheless important. To create a truly high quality e-commerce site, the company believes, your goods need to be coupled with the best in customer care. So Foofoo emphasizes superior customer service with a "no questions asked" return policy and extended calling hours. In addition, the Web site uses best-of-breed technology backed by an extensive order-monitoring and tracking system in order to make shopping as convenient as possible.

In the end, Foofoo is banking on the belief that the Internet is the clear paradigm for doing business in the future. "I want to be a part of making that happen. It's truly an exciting prospect," says Ling.

"The first time I saw a Web page, I realized that here was something that could go a long way toward leveling the playing field between big and small companies," she adds. "Foofoo can offer just as much in the way of functionality and 'look and feel' as a multimillion-dollar corporation can. The Internet seems to be virgin territory for big and small companies, and all of us realize that the ubiquitous nature of the Net levels the playing field.... Right now, the Internet space is anyone's game."

Ling has done an incredible job getting Foofoo.com ready to capitalize on the capabilities provided by the Internet. Starting an Internet company is unlike anything else in the world, although Ling notes, "Having had a baby, I can tell you that launching a Web site is a close second in the 'birthing' department, and I've most certainly bonded with the baby Foofoo.com. Neither experience has left me with much time for personal reflection." A common trait among Internet entrepreneurs, including Ling, is to be "wired," or as Ling notes, "I'm embarrassed to say that I have seven numbers for voice mails, one laptop, three desktop PCs, and one pager. Being the First Foo, I am absolutely determined to fit into one of the Foofoo quiz categories, and I don't want to pick that picture of people on phones in their cars." Clearly, she is ready for all that comes her way.

## What Is Foofoo?

The Foofoo.com team spent six months coming up with their name. Despite countless meetings and days' worth of time defending and explaining the Foofoo.com name and other topics, they finally finalized their name and business model. "Idiocy prevailed, our sense of humor is still intact, and the name is here to stay," notes Ling. The funny part is, she adds, "My mother did not 'get' the name. My best friend from college did not 'get' the name. Former business associates thought that I had lost my mind. You should see the first—and for that matter, second—reactions we get from prospective hires. And then there were the incredibly blank looks from my fellow airplane travelers who surreptitiously stole looks at my luggage tags. They must have thought I was in the business of racy, um, underwear!" notes Ling. However, in the world of the Internet, you need to get surfers to remember your Web address. Could you ever forget a name like Foofoo?

The importance of creating an identifiable brand name on the Internet is key. Companies such as Yahoo!

and Amazon.com have such far-reaching brands because they have unique names that individuals now associate with the products and services they offer. Building a brand from scratch is never an easy process. It involves lots of media, devoted users, and most important, a lot of cash. There is also the chance that the wrong connotation for your brand will begin to develop against your own wish.

Developing brand recognition and fine-tuning your revenue model are other important parts of turning an idea into reality. Foofoo's brand-building strategy began simply by choosing an impossible-to-forget, easy-to-spell name. And it has worked to leverage that name to the fullest extent possible. Its motto, "Are you Foofoo?" has appeared in numerous places, in particular on other Web sites such as USA Today, iBeauty, and Egghead. The company has also arranged print campaigns with some of its commerce and content partners, including Sky Guide, Healing Retreats and Spas, Departures, and American Express. Offline events and linking its brand with other premium names (mainly content partners such as *Elle, Men's Health,* and *Food & Wine*) have also helped to reach out to customers no matter where they are.

According to Ling, "Foofoo is about fulfilling your desire for high quality, high experience, extreme style, and premium brands. Foofoo is about fun. It's about feeling better, more entertained, sexier, smarter, and less stressed." You are Foofoo if:

- You work hard and play harder, but more important, you work and play fair.
- You appreciate high quality, new experiences, and fabulous service.

- You are passionate about something—anything!
- You take care of yourself and those around you.
- You indulge yourself and others, simply because you and they are worth it.
- You are constantly working to embody all these traits.

Of course, developing this exact image for a brand takes a lot more than just writing it down on paper. Every interaction a consumer has with your name, product, or service will develop the customer's image of a brand. This is an important challenge for every Internet company, and especially for Foofoo.

---

### Foofoo.com's Key Success Factors

- Implementing a "no questions asked" return policy and extended calling hours
- Using best-of-breed technology backed by an extensive order-monitoring and tracking system
- Learning from advisory board members' experiences and avoiding potential pitfalls by asking many questions of them
- Finding partners who add to the company's financial well-being and its expertise, relationships, or delivery speed
- Participating in offline events and linking its brand with other premium names known among consumers

---

## MAKING IT HAPPEN

The first step in building an Internet company is finding capital. Financing has been tough for Foofoo and continues to be somewhat of a struggle. The company's main financing has come from private investors. So far, this has been sufficient because Foofoo's business model isn't terribly cash-intensive as far as Internet start-ups go.

Most partners, both strategic and financial, wanted equity in Foofoo, but few were willing to bring cash to the table. Foofoo has done few deals that include equity, however. This is because most partners ended up being willing to work with the company and leverage its other assets in one way or another.

> *"Money is money, but money with experience, connections, and clout is The Money."*

Ling suspects that it's easier to find capital if you're developing a tools-based implementation, a category e-commerce player (e.g., books or CDs), or a Web-based development or consulting service. Foofoo's model is a bit different, and although Ling says most consumers tend to "get it," some venture capitalists think that the company is trying to compete with specific category e-commerce players. Despite this incorrect understanding, Foofoo has been able to raise enough cash to support its needs to date, and its venture capital efforts haven't been all-consuming for senior management, as that process often tends to be. The company is also finding that it is easier to get capital now that it is actually up and running and is rapidly developing its user base.

"When it comes right down to it, we're more interested in finding partners who add to our financial well-being and our expertise, relationships, or delivery speed," says Ling. "Money is money, but money with experience, connections, and clout is The Money."

It is never easy making the jump to start an Internet company. Notes Ling, "I took the family nest egg and invested it in something in which I ardently believe—Foofoo.com. I am either one smart cookie or one crazy kook. I believe that I'm a smart cookie, because I am Foofoo. Confidence is a vital part of being Foofoo. You simply cannot get happier, healthier, wealthier, better looking, less stressed, or sexier without it. I believe that I'm doing the smart thing because there are a lot of Foofoo people out there who are looking for an oasis on the Internet." The first step is always the hardest, but once you take it you are on your way.

According to Ling, "I'm a big advocate of experiencing both the big and the small. After all, one helps give you perspective on the other, vantages you wouldn't have necessarily noticed individually. For me, working at IBM Corp. helped me fortify my values of integrity and honesty in the workplace, regardless of what the competition might be doing. I've carried those values with me from large workplace to small and hold dear the fact that I can also see them in the Foofoo.com team. I applaud when I see others in the dot-com world doing the same."

The next step in starting an Internet company is finding the right talent. The majority of Foofoo's managers are its founders, all of whom know each other through other ventures. As for the rest of the staff, "We've been lucky," says Ling. "We have a great recruiting firm working for us. We've been able to tap into resources from past jobs and acquaintances. The skill sets we need, especially combining fashion and the Internet, are sometimes hard to find, but in the early stages of a start-up, it's a matter

of finding driven, dedicated people who will give it everything they've got.

"Working for an Internet start-up is a hot ticket
these days, so getting people interested is not the problem," she adds. "The big issue is knowing what talent is
needed and then finding people who can come in and
make an immediate impact. Our policy has been to not
skimp when it comes to filling positions. If there's a need,
we'll fill it with someone qualified, regardless of the cost."

The most difficult part is finding good technical people who know their area of expertise without going
through extensive training. The technology behind the
Internet, especially with complicated Web sites, is such a
new phenomenon that it is hard to find people with years
of technical experience.

### Approach to Personnel Management

Employees are almost all twentysomethings who view the
work environment as "controlled chaos." Foofoo looks for
employees who "will uphold the values of integrity and honesty that are so integral to the success of any organization."
The dress code is casual, and the atmosphere is fun, but
everyone knows that it's a place to work, and there's a performance-based compensation system. Incentives include
stock, cash, and free drinks.

When looking at the Foofoo team, Ling is surprised by
the diversity of the group. Every employee has such a different background, yet they all tie together well. It is so
important to have a diverse set of skills so that opportunities, problems, and daily operations can be viewed from

different perspectives. Most important, Ling looks for employees who "will uphold the same values of integrity and honesty that are so integral to the success of any organization; people who are committed to each other in the pursuit of a common goal."

Foofoo's primary source of revenue is consumer retail. It currently has more than 500 commerce partners, and its revenue model is based heavily on a percentage of the sales of products sold on the site. Additional revenues are expected to come from advertising and sponsorship. At present, there is no charge for membership to the site, but Foofoo is evaluating the merits of tiering membership by benefits. Eventually, there may be a charge for the top levels of membership.

## Most Unique Approach to Management

CEO Ling advocates changing team dynamics by changing the physical setting. The pride and joy is the informal setting of the Living Room, a corner of the office that has a couch, a few chairs, pillows, some whiteboards and a water-trickling, Zen-like, mind-calming fountain. "Meetings have been different since we started having them in the Living Room. The ideas are better, the conversations are clearer, and the dialogue is more animated."

A key to Foofoo's moving beyond the idea stage has been its advisory board. This board is comprised of experts in every area the site touches on—e-commerce, marketing, sales, and publishing. Foofoo deliberately chose its advisory board members from different backgrounds to ensure a variety of views, opinions, and expertise. The board gives advice about both long- and short-term strat-egy and introduces Foofoo staff to appropriate contacts in their industries. Learning from board members' own experiences and avoiding potential pitfalls by asking many questions has proved invaluable.

## GROWING PAINS

Any start-up company faces a number of obstacles and risks in its infancy. Obviously, the biggest risk is the chance that the company won't succeed. Many of Foo-foo's employees gave up opportunities to work at much larger and more established companies in order to be at Foofoo. That's not something that the staff dwells on, however. Everyone is totally committed to making the company a success. "None of us are making other plans," says Ling. "In the end, we will make Foofoo succeed be-cause we don't have a plan B."

A more unexpected obstacle involved development of the site's technology. Most of the people on Foofoo's man-agement team have high-tech backgrounds and thought that managing this piece would be easy. They contracted out to a friendly firm with whom they had a strong rela-tionship, but the management of that firm changed in the middle of Foofoo's launch. Changes in management, sub-sequent employee turnovers, and lack of commitment on the firm's part caused heartburn for Foofoo.

Legally, the major obstacles centered on the particu-lars of the company's name. The founders wanted to use "Foofoo," but only if the URL was available and they could trademark the name. The trademarking process, which they expected to be complicated, ended up being easy. Getting the URL was tougher. Someone already owned the Foofoo domain name. The company ended up sending its most charming team member to do some sweet talking, and he was eventually successful in acquiring the URL (for not even a couple hundred dollars).

---

### Bottom Line: Is Foofoo.com Profitable Yet?

Foofoo's main goal is to grow revenue and increase its shareholders' worth, but being a very young company, its primary concern is driving as much traffic as possible to the site. Traffic growth has been steady and exciting. For the first three months after the site's launch, traffic was driven almost solely by word-of-mouth and media coverage in major newspapers (e.g., *Washington Post, The New York Times, The Wall Street Journal*) and local TV news. There are many ways to measure a firm's growth, and sales revenue is just one. As long as the back-end processes are in place (and the right mix of products and content is on the site), Foofoo believes the revenue will come.

---

A series of focus groups about eight months after the site's launch revealed some unexpected problems as well. The first focus group provided insight into how Foofoo could improve from a design perspective. People simply didn't like the look and feel of the site. This reaction, combined with feedback received through e-mail, convinced Foofoo to redesign the site's layout. Focus groups were also used to test a large number of potential products. The idea was to see how consumers ranked them on the "Foofoo scale" (i.e., how unique and high quality they were perceived to be).

Foofoo also found that its lack of previous brand and infrastructure was both a strength and weakness. While it didn't have much to rely on in terms of brick-and-mortar or established business processes, it could build the company so that it was specifically tailored to the Internet-based medium. And while it wasn't an established brand, it could compete in the marketplace by leveraging established brands with the Foofoo name.

Another pleasant surprise came in the form of business development efforts and responses from potential employees. While building partnerships wasn't easy, Foofoo received good responses from many of the companies it approached. Even though it was a small start-up, many of the established firms treated it like a peer. And Foofoo got, and continues to get, hundreds of unsolicited résumés from highly qualified people who go to great lengths to describe why they are "Foofoo." The company has a 100 percent acceptance rate for all job offers so far.

> ### Advice to Other Internet Entrepreneurs
>
> The most challenging aspect of running an Internet business is prioritization and remaining focused on the reason you started the business in the first place.

## FOOFOO FUN

Foofoo employees describe their work environment as "controlled chaos." Most staff members work in a large, open area, grouped more or less by function. At first this environment worried some people (who were used to having their own offices), but it has turned out to be a re-sounding success. Whereas in a traditional office you have to walk down the hall to check if someone is available if you want to grab his or her ear about a matter, in Foofoo's office you can see when someone is free, or just shout out a quick question. Instant messaging has also proven to be a valuable communication device.

While a great deal of noise can sometimes result from this arrangement, it has a purpose, and employees enjoy the atmosphere. They say it is a fun place to work. Something is always going on, and company lunch, dinners, and happy hours are common.

In fact, at Foofoo.com they stopped using their conference room a long time ago. According to Ling, "There is actually a rumor around the office that some employees have never actually sat around our twelve-foot table, endlessly fidgeting and fighting off ennui." Instead, Foofoo.com has a special place called the Living Room where they hold their meetings. The Living Room is a corner of the office that has a couch and a few chairs, a few whiteboards, and a water-trickling, Zen-like, mind-calming fountain. The setting is informal, and they have more than a few cushions should anyone choose to sit on the floor.

Ling notes, "Our meetings have been different since we started having them in the Living Room. The ideas are better, the conversations are clearer, and the dialogue is more animated. No matter what the topic or how heated the debate, the communication between team members is better. I've become a big advocate of changing team dynamics by changing the physical setting. Remember how much fun it was in high school when you got to hold class outside? Our last office location had lots of individual of-

fices; this new office has lots of open space. Guess what?
The team dynamics changed. I'm thinking about giving
away our big conference table and creating a den in our
conference room space. Anyone need a twelve-foot ma-
hogany behemoth? In the meantime, try setting up a living room in your office. I'd be interested to hear if you
think your meetings start getting a little more . . . well,
Foofoo."

Not having a storefront has no adverse effects, either.
Foofoo has frequent visitors to the office (e.g., investors,
board members, advisers) and therefore must maintain a
high degree of professionalism at all times. The dress
code is casual, and the atmosphere is fun, but everyone
knows that this is a place to work.

It helps that the company offers a lot of incentives:
"Stock, cash, free drinks, and belief in the vision," quips
Ling. Foofoo operates on a performance-based compensation system, and part of the culture is to encourage
hard work through proper rewards (be they promotions,
raises, or stock options). Stock is probably the primary
motivator; knowing that hard work today could lead to
big bucks down the road makes the company fly.

## PRIORITIES, PRIORITIES, PRIORITIES

Foofoo believes that the most challenging (and one of the
most important) aspects of running an Internet business
is prioritization. There are so many ideas floating around,
so many great partnering opportunities, so many
thoughts on features to add to the site, says Ling. Sifting
through all of these things (and determining what is truly
essential to build the company) is a constant challenge.

Ling also notes you should have a clear plan of attack and measurable goals for success. And once the goals are set, give "everything you have to achieve them."

When its founders started Foofoo, they had a clear understanding of what they wanted: to create "an oasis of quality on the Internet for the upwardly mobile consumer." That vision has not changed, but the plan for how it will be delivered is continually tweaked and molded. Each day, the company is presented with ideas and opportunities that could add value to its vision. But a small team of people only has so many hours in the day and can only handle so many tasks. In selecting which ideas to execute, it's critical to make sure that you have the resources in place to allow them to succeed. And it's important to know what you are giving up in order to make something new happen.

As with starting any business, it's a constant juggling act to find the right elements to make your company successful. After over a year at Foofoo, Ling's best piece of advice is: "Don't lose focus. The reason you started a business in the first place was for a reason that was very clear when beginning. Every day, remind yourself what that focus is and make sure you don't lose sight of it, no matter what business challenges and opportunities arise. Prioritizing your opportunities will consume a lot of time, but if you know what the focus is, the task is much easier."

Ling even contributes certain introspective articles to the site. For example, in the excerpt of an article reprinted here, Ling lends insight into her own life for the Foofoo.com readers and a nice welcome to new members—a nice personal touch for the CEO of an Internet company.

### Sandwiched?
### Connie Ling

Let me be clear that this article is not about food, although I will admit to a very healthy passion for fabulous food of any sort in large quantities. Instead, I use this term to characterize many of my generation who are pulled in two directions by the familial demands of both parents and children. I think the term *sandwiched* is appropriate to refer to being crushed for personal time while caring for aging parents and growing children.

Most days, I know that I'm lucky. Although I recently lost my mother, my dad is still around, and so are my in-laws. My husband and child are healthy, as am I. Still, I worry about the physical distance between everyone in my family. It's exceedingly difficult to provide additional care for a loved one when they're far away, as my mother was when she finally succumbed to cancer.

Many of us are also "sandwiched" between other demands and obligations that compete for our attentions. You might be straddling work and marriage, or finances and friendships. Whatever it is, your struggle is equally as significant.

With that in mind, I'd like to build onto the definition of "Foofoo." We say that being Foofoo is having an affinity for the fun and finer things in life, a willingness to indulge in the best life has to offer. But being Foofoo is also taking the time for yourself to do whatever pleases you. We strive to make Foofoo.com an oasis on the Internet. It's a place that allows us, the "sand-wiched" ones, to enjoy ourselves even for a few precious moments. Whether you use Foofoo.com as a means by which to relax, or a portal to find the products, services, and information that will help you to relax, Foofoo.com is an indulgence for those in need. We make sure you know what's new, what's been done, what's hot, and what's not—even if you never, ever get a chance to just sit on your couch and turn on the TV.

Take a deep breath. Relax, enjoy. Even for a brief moment.

And, on behalf of my team, welcome to Foofoo.com. © Foofoo.com.

## BUILDING A HAPPY CUSTOMER BASE

It's important to Foofoo to establish a loyal base of users, a community of people who come to the site frequently. In this vein, the site offers interactive elements, such as message boards, online chats, and a "Daily Quiz," all of which are popular features.

The Daily Quiz in particular has seen explosive growth in terms of page visits. The Quiz was actually an established Internet humor and trivia site when Foofoo acquired it in September 1999. Visitors can now answer light trivia questions (and read others' responses) while they shop.

The acquisition of the Daily Quiz was done in con-junction with a total redesign of the site and an extensive (and expensive) advertising campaign with *USA Today*. Site traffic increased almost 300 percent overnight. On the surface, these numbers looked fantastic. But Foofoo makes a clear distinction between "visitors" (those people who come to the site and look around) and "shoppers" (people who have filled out the registration form and are set up to begin purchasing from Foofoo). The company's greatest challenge is to convert all visitors to shoppers.

Another one of Foofoo's priorities that is especially worth noting is customer feedback. The company puts user satisfaction at the top of its list. Site look and feel, ease of use, and quality of content are all areas in which the company relies a great deal on feedback from its shoppers. The initial site design, for example, prompted many shoppers to let Foofoo know that they hated its color scheme. "Too much pink!" was the general consensus. The numbers were such that Foofoo could conclude that this was a definite opinion among users. This feeling was reinforced in focus groups, where a clear majority of participants expressed dislike of the color scheme, which let to the complete redesign of the site. This coincided with the launch of Foofoo's biggest ad campaign, and since then, feedback has swung in the other direction, with most shoppers enthusiastic about the new look and feel.

To get this valuable feedback, Foofoo provides multiple ways for customers to contact the company. Phone numbers are posted on the site, and users can send e-mail to "Feedback," "Editor," and "Customer Care." The company also scans all of the message boards for those posts that require a response. Ling even notes in one of her articles, "I'm asking you, the members of the Foofoo. com community, to send us your ideas and requests about what's on your list this holiday season. I'm asking a little bit early, I know, but we want to do our best to bring those items to our shopping pages in time for you to be able to give frequently to your friends and family—and so that you may give frequently to yourself! And if you're a manufacturer and you've got a product that you'd like us to try, send it on over! We're pretty open to new experiences over here at Foofoo.com headquarters—which is all part of being Foofoo—and we're willing to give most things a test drive (those little Audi TTs are looking kind of cute)." This is called *personalization*—and Foofoo.com is doing it very well.

---

### Vision of the New Economy

Today we build Internet sites for use on computers, but soon we'll be pushing into cell phones, handhelds, and televisions. The day when the Internet can be speedily and readily available in every home over a television set is when it will be an undeniable moneymaker, since companies will be able to truly reach out to the public at large and allow them to quickly and easily access information when they need it. Companies with key infrastructure technologies such as Akamai (content distribution and caching), Ask Jeeves (improved search engines), and iContact (real-time interactive chat) will also be key to enhancing the online user experience.

---

## PLANS FOR THE FUTURE

Foofoo's main objective continues to be "to own" affluent spenders online. It wants to be *the* place people go on the Web to support a work-hard, play-hard lifestyle, to experience new things, and to purchase high-quality goods and services.

On the business front, the company plans to go public, probably in less than three years. Its growth objectives as measured in revenue are aggressive. By the end of 2000, it expects to exceed its 1999 numbers more than fourfold. The company currently has fifteen employees, and expects to be have forty by year-end 2000 and up to 100 or 150 by the end of 2001.

Objectives for site traffic are fairly aggressive as well and reflect hopes for results from the company's robust marketing campaign. The goal is to get 10,000 unique visits to the site each day by the end of 1999 and to have 50,000 registered Foofoo members.

Right now, the site offers the ability for anyone anywhere to purchase products and have them shipped to any international address. The company doesn't have a site based in any language besides English at this point, although it's something Foofoo will consider doing in the future.

As far as hopes and worries for the future, Foofoo thinks the worst thing that could happen to the Internet industry in terms of the effect on its business (besides servers crashing) would be for it to remain a PC-focused medium. The major limiting factor of the Internet right now is that it's "technical." You have to boot up your PC, dial in, hook up wires, and so on. "If we can't make it easier, it'll never gain mass acceptance," says Ling.

Consequently, Foofoo's number-one wish is for the Internet to be speedily and readily available in every home over a television set. If companies can truly reach out to the public at large and allow them to quickly and easily access information when they need it, the Internet will be an undeniable moneymaker. Foofoo's business thrives on making a connection with its members, so the more people it can reach out to, and the easier its interactions with them are, the more successful it will be.

## A WORLD ON THE WEB

Creating a company in the midst of a constantly changing industry has given Foofoo a distinct perspective on the Internet and where it's headed. The Web provides customers with convenience and variety that simply isn't possible through traditional means.

Foofoo's employees, almost all twentysomethings, use the Internet for just about everything in their daily lives. Many of them no longer receive a newspaper at home. Why should they? They can read the *Washington Post* and a dozen other good papers online. They can get AP reports all day long, look up movie reviews and show times, find directions to anywhere they're going, and book flights. It's absolutely indispensable to them. Online businesses they use most include Expedia, Amazon, CDNow, E\*TRADE, Drugstore.com, Liquor by Wire, and JCrew.

In fact, Foofoo.com employees have been known for their energy in promoting their company. Rumor has it that Foofoo.com employees have been spotted "accosting" people in elevators, asking them, "Are you Foofoo?" Ling responds to the lighthearted accusations: "The reactions have been varied. Some folks have engaged in a subsequent, 'I am interested'-type dialogue, while others pretended that they didn't even hear the question. Instead, they stared fixedly at the floor numbers as the elevator moved—sort of the way you and I would behave if a stranger got too close to us in a big, otherwise empty elevator. Are we nuts? Actually, I think that we are pretty normal, but I'm undoubtedly biased. I believe that when normal individuals become absolutely passionate about something, they start doing some unusual things. I think it's pretty darn cool—um, I mean, Foofoo—to care enough about something to express that passion loudly, visually, physically, for God and all the world to see."

Being in the Internet business also allows the Foofoo staff to closely observe what's going on around them. One company they respect immensely (based just a few miles away from Foofoo in northern Virginia) is America On-line.

"I have to admire what AOL has managed to do," says Ling. "They're the biggest, they're among the oldest, and yet they still manage to deliver a lowest-common-denominator service to the masses. At the end of the day, it's not about how cool it is; it's whether it works and it's easy. AOL does that very well."

She also mentions Akamai, which she thinks may be a revolutionary player in the Internet space. Akamai offers a service that caches Web pages at various points around the globe, making it easier to distribute content around the world very quickly. The need for caching has come to the forefront because it offers benefits such as reducing bandwidth consumption and essentially brings content closer to the user requesting the information, thereby reducing errors in data transmission and allowing for faster information download. As the technology catches on, it will increase volumes of traffic on the Internet while enhancing the user experience with increased graphic, video, and audio content.

Other Foofoo favorites include Peapod, Ask Jeeves, and iContact. Peapod is an online grocery store that offers a simple but extensive shopping system and provides home delivery. Ask Jeeves, a search engine that allows people to phrase queries in regular sentence form (instead of through search words), takes a slightly new approach to searching the Web, and its capabilities should get better with time. One of the big disappointments of the Internet industry is that search technology has not improved that much in five years. Ask Jeeves could change that. Technology from iContact allows real-time interactive chat with customer service representatives. It operates through a Web browser while the user is on the site. It's just like being in a retail store and asking a clerk for help. The software engages the user and allows them to interact with customer service representatives while moving through the site, helping the Web truly be a one-to-one experience.

Foofoo also thinks the incorporation of video into Web content, and by extension into Web advertising, is inevitable. The company has been following the advances being made in the streaming media industry and is excited about the capabilities. It believes the Web will one day be as ubiquitous as television. Unlike television, though, the Web will afford users the opportunity to interact with and take control of the ads they see. Wouldn't it be nice, when you see a commercial for a car on television, to be able to freeze the picture, zoom in on the tires, open the doors, listen to the engine, or go back and see the price again? The enabling technology is already in place, and it won't be long before bandwidth issues are resolved, making these ads as common as today's banners.

Getting people to pay attention to ads is, of course, another story. Many people change the radio station 90 percent of the time when a commercial comes on. Web advertising isn't much different. Foofoo believes that it's not the advertisements themselves that people avoid; it's advertisements for products they aren't interested in. This is why there is such a thing as targeted advertising. There's no secret behind why you don't see many professional wrestling commercials during *Days of Our Lives*.

The Web offers the unique opportunity for companies to target their ads not just to specific markets (e.g., soap opera watchers), but also to specific individuals. Foofoo, for example, can gather a great deal of information about visitors to its site, including demographic information, shopping history, most frequently visited pages, referring Web sites, and where visitors go when they leave. It can then use that information to make sure people won't see advertisements they aren't interested in. When Joe Smith logs onto Foofoo, he won't just see ads targeted to a white male age 30 to 35. He'll see ads targeted to Joe Smith.

Clearly, the Internet is transforming the landscape of business and creating new opportunities. It's not just a craze, says Ling. "For better or worse, the Internet will become as much a part of our everyday life as television, radio, or the telephone. In fact, it will most likely incorporate all three of those tools. It is a revolutionary medium that will prove to be one of the identifying characteristics of our generation," she adds. "I love the technology that makes it happen, I love developing the vehicle to reach out to consumers, and I love thinking about all of the things we can do as a company to make our vision a reality. Some people have jobs; others are lucky enough to have a career. I feel as if I have something entirely different: I have the opportunity to be involved in building a brand and a service that can reach people more effectively than any other medium on the planet. That's worth getting out of bed for in the morning.

"I can't wait to see how our company and the medium evolves in the years ahead. Today, we're building an Internet site for use on computers. Soon, we may be pushing our service to cell phones, handhelds, and televisions. The possibilities are endless, and there's no place I'd rather be to watch it all happen."

*As of publication of this book, questions have arisen regarding the state of Foofoo.com and where they are heading, and the company's officials have been unavailable, so far, for comment on these issues.*

# 10

# HIWIRE

*An inside look at HIWIRE's successful quest to secure capital, form an elite advisory board, and capitalize on the powerful communications capabilities of the Internet*

Radio stations on the Web appeal to a wide cross-section of the public, and the reach of their programming is an advertiser's dream. Digitoy Entertainment, Inc. (a.k.a. "HIWIRE") wants to become the dominant force in the online radio advertising industry. Founded in October 1997 and located in downtown Los Angeles, HIWIRE distributes Internet radio tuners to Webcasters in exchange for valuable audience measurement data that these tuners collect.

## *Fast-Track Facts*

| | |
|---|---|
| **Cofounders** | Jim Pavilak and James Lambert |
| **Business Model** | Infrastructure software (Internet radio tuners) and streaming ad insertion service; revenue comes from Internet radio broadcasts paying for audio ads |
| **Funding** | Angel investors |
| **Business Partners** | OEMs, domestic and international ISPs, and companies with complementary applications (e.g., MusicMatch MP3 player) |
| **Target Customers** | Internet radio broadcasters (i.e., Webcasters) |

## THE CONCEPT

Jim Pavilak and James Lambert were digital toy designers and producers when they came up with the idea for HIWIRE. At the time, they were brainstorming about affordable toys that would do something fun with the Internet, this for their digital toy publisher. The idea for a stand-alone Internet radio tuner, which allows you to play audio on your computer, came out of this mission. They had a working demo the day after they came up with the idea, and the day after that, took it to their publisher as another "cybertoy" option. The publisher expressed much interest, but over the course of the next couple months announced that it was getting out of the software business entirely. By this point, Pavilak and Lambert had already realized that they could make a much more lucrative deal—and give up much less control and ownership to a publisher—if they found the right angel investors and developed the idea into a business. So they set out to find a "tech angel."

"We didn't originally set out with the idea to start a business—we got involved in this as a way to provide a simple solution," says Pavilak. "We were driven by the desire to make cool technology simple to use, deceptively simple." They wanted to make accessing the vast universe of content on the Internet "so easy to do that it would seem obvious" and would be taken for granted. "Computers are such a pain in the ass that it's almost impossible to take them for granted," Pavilak says.

He initially explained the radio tuner to Lambert as an under-$50 piece of hardware that would let you use two buttons to access a database of all of the Webcasting stations around the world, which number in the hundreds. The stations "would just play music," without forcing the user to sift through layers of Web pages, which not only takes up time but provides ample opportunities to get lost along the way. Lambert quickly pointed out that they probably didn't want to be in the hardware business, so the two of them began developing a software configurable online radio tuning solution. First, they wrote a pitch paragraph on what their product would do and where the opportunity was (which eventually evolved into a business plan). Then Lambert plopped himself in front of his computer and had a working demo and a first run at an interface by the next morning.

This is how it works: HIWIRE is a desktop Internet audio tuner that allows listeners to tune into almost every radio station available on the Web. Netcasters, in turn, are given the opportunity to sell local ads that match with listeners' zip codes and other vector information. Since over 80 percent of radio ads are local, this gives every participating netcaster a way to turn itself into a kind of network. Each station's content can be supported by local listeners, similar to the model that TV networks use with their affiliates.

What if, for example, an AM broadcaster in the pine forests of South Georgia has an idea for a radio drama show to simulcast to the Internet? The broadcaster can set up a server and start to broadcast anywhere. Listeners in Seattle might love the program, but the broadcaster has to pay for every listener's connection, and "things are going to get stale quickly if the broadcaster can't at least buy canned beans and instant espresso," explains Pavilak. "There's no point in soliciting the local catfish farms for ads; they already put in a fifteen-second spot just because they like the show—plus, who in Seattle cares about the price of catfish in Georgia? The broadcaster doesn't have the time or staff to solicit any national ads. Enter HIWIRE."

HIWIRE returns the data on listenership for each station, even if there is only one listener. It could find out that there is a twenty-eight-year-old male in Seattle who listens to the show every other Tuesday, for instance. And a local cookware supplier in Seattle might want to mount a campaign directed at men under thirty who listen to radio drama. HIWIRE could then take out the catfish ad and put in the cookware ad at the appropriate time.

Thus, the station provides the airtime, the retailer provides the ad, and they don't even need to know one another to reach the target audience. HIWIRE believes that for radio stations and all broadcasters, this capability is the key to making money on the Internet. Since HIWIRE takes a placement fee for each inserted ad, it stands to make significant revenue from this model as well. Right now, the company is working closely with terrestrial broadcasters as they move to the Web, as well as with traditional advertisers. Its presence is represented primarily at non-Internetcentric conferences related to those industries.

The mechanism that HIWIRE has developed works for any streaming media content, but founders Pavilak and Lambert like radio for two main reasons. First, Pavilak considers radio to be true "theater of the mind" entertainment. "You can enjoy it on an active or passive level. You can follow a radio show and drive a car or work—try to do that with video entertainment—or you can turn off the lights and let your brain open up to the audio way beyond what the best TV can offer." He uses the example of *Star Wars, the Original Audio Drama* tape or compact disc to illustrate his point. "Almost everyone has seen the movie, but the people who then listen to the radio show [which has a slightly different story] say they can't believe the 'visuals' that occur."

### HIWIRE's Key Success Factors

- Getting "the right money" from partners who can significantly improve the company's chance of success
- Focusing on distribution rather than marketing
- Hiring a "small army of legal advisers" to handle the issues surrounding getting financing
- Having a good advisory board that is a constant source of ideas and inspiration, not to mention contacts

The second reason Pavilak and Lambert pursued audio is because of the practical matter of the bandwidth limitations that continue to exist. "Eventually, we may be able to get uncompressed digital video feeds into our wrist-watches," he says, "but right now and for the next few years, it's going to be expensive to get more than a tiny, low-resolution image to most desktops. For our megabits of entertainment value, we'll take radio anytime."

## THE EXECUTION

HIWIRE is not the first business that its founders have started. "We're both chronic entrepreneurial cases," says Pavilak. "I started my first real business in my teens, sold it when I was thirty, and have always worked hard on some scheme or another. I'm proud to say that I haven't held a real job since puberty." Lambert has founded businesses ranging from a successful theater company to a company that invented and produced a special mouse feeder used in labs for scientific research. "Neither of us takes the easy route through the maze," laughs Pavilak.

Neither of them set out to start an Internet radio business, either. It's just that "we were both driven by a passion for a good interface, which may sound hokey but it's the truth," says Pavilak. They knew that most frustrations people come up against online are the result of a run-in with some poorly thought out user interface. Both of them were intrigued by the possibilities presented by computers and wanted to create products that brought the enjoyable aspects of what you could do with them "up to the surface, where mere mortals could get at them," says Pavilak. "We were on a mission to clear as much of the smoke-and-mirrors complexity of computers away by developing easier ways to access the fun parts. This go-around we didn't start as businesspeople. We were simply pursuing what interested us and in the process came across an irresistible opportunity."

Even though he thinks there has probably never been an easier time to raise money, Pavilak still says that finding financing was tough. It's important to get "the right money," from partners who can significantly improve your company's chance of success. Pavilak thinks that perhaps he and Lambert were too early at first. "While you might think it's a huge advantage to have no perceived competitor building castles in the same sandbox, I believe that it actually makes it harder to get the first money in," he explains. "When there are other notable successes out there, it makes it easier for investors to get a sense of the size of the potential market and it helps to validate your idea . . . ."

When HIWIRE first went after money, there was simply no business category for online radio, and since the space had not been validated, potential investors would ask a lot of questions, beginning with, "Why would anyone want to listen to radio over the Internet?" Months later, after Broadcast.com went public, the "why" questions eased up and became, "How can you compete with Broadcast.com, or some other well-funded effort?" "When the questions start turning from why to how are you going to implement it, you are in the home stretch," says Pavilak. "This means that they understand the opportunity and need convincing that you are the team to pull it off."

The person who turned out to be HIWIRE's first angel investor overheard Pavilak describing the idea to a friend of his in the locker room of the Hollywood YMCA. "Sitting there on the bench, he interrupted with questions that rose in intensity," says Pavilak. "Soon it became clear that he was in the game of seeding tech companies. With the blink of an eye and a mere six months of intense due diligence, we closed our first round of angel funding."

After that, the company decided to take the millions of dollars that it could have spent on a consumer marketing campaign and put it into direct business and product development. Since HIWIRE's first goal is to garner as much distribution as possible—"and we didn't have a spare $50 million to educate and entice people to come to our site and download," as Pavilak puts it—it flipped around the usual business plan for Internet start-ups.

Instead of branding or marketing to consumers at this point, HIWIRE is concentrating on forming partnerships with popular sites, mostly computer manufacturers and Internet service providers (ISPs), to create cobranded radio tuners. These sites distribute the tuners to their loyal customer bases. Through these partnerships, HIWIRE has been able to get millions of tuners onto computer desktops throughout the world. "We created a product that provides value to other popular consumer branded businesses," says Pavilak. The company's only marketing expense, if it can be called that, is the attendance of selected industry conferences. It's at these conferences that the company develops most of its partnerships, which in turn provide its distribution.

The success of this distribution strategy relies mostly on aggressively partnering with major original equipment manufacturers (OEMs), complementary desktop applications, domestic and international ISPs, and other companies that are interested in having their brand appear as a desktop icon. HIWIRE provides a benefit to partners who are marketing to specific target groups, especially since there is so much competition in the Internet industry for consumer attention. Thus, companies bear a huge cost-to-market through conventional means; HIWIRE believes that partnering is a more cost-efficient and effective way to reach large audiences.

This philosophy seems to have paid off. For two years, the company consisted of two guys selling an idea and working from their homes. Now HIWIRE has a large Los Angeles office and satellite locations in San Francisco and New York, as well as over a dozen highly skilled software engineers and relationships with prominent radio groups. And its distribution agreements number in the tens of millions.

## Advice to Other Internet Entrepreneurs

- Be prepared to spend about 20 percent of your time recruiting, once your basic crew and management team is in place.
- Stick with the vision and have the courage to follow it through. "Tenacity is an incredibly important resource."
- Align yourself with strong lawyers who know the territory and can get drafts done in "Internet time." Otherwise, be prepared for the time, attention, documentation, and cost of the many legal issues associated with starting a business.
- Continue to move your company forward and get all of your deals done before they go out of date.
- Find the balance between patience and passion that you'll need to survive this process. Once you've gotten your idea off the ground, have the confidence to delegate and turn over responsibility; that is the only way to grow.

## The Details

In HIWIRE's experience, it can be difficult to find good talent for an Internet start-up until you find the right key people—a CEO, a CTO, and a strong business development person. Then, it gets much easier. According to Pavilak, this is because top people know and attract top talent. "If you have a compelling idea and a good management team, top people will be pounding on your doors," he says." Everyone in the western hemisphere knows that there is simply no sexier business or quicker way to get rich at the moment than being a part of a promising Internet start-up." Consequently, HIWIRE was stunned by the caliber of talent and résumés that somehow found their way to its door. But "to get the initial team in place requires that you identify the individuals, and actually pitch them with the same, if not more, passion and intensity that you would a VC," he cautions. "You must sell them on your vision. Passion is contagious."

HIWIRE found its management team in a number of different ways. Pavilak and Lambert had been producing software for several years when they started the company, so they had a good resource pool to start with. They also worked with an agent early on who introduced them to several CEO candidates, as well to as a number of business development people.

The CEO they chose, Warren Schlichting, has spent the past nine years working with a number of start-up companies in a range of industries, including Stratamodel, a Houston-based 3-D petroleum software company; Camden Asset Management, a market-neutral hedge fund; and Yucatan Foods, a branded specialty food company. In all three cases, Schlichting became involved before the companies had any revenues and worked with their founders to develop long-term strategies, assemble a team, and build a viable company. He also developed successful exit strategies yielding attractive returns in two of the three cases. Prior to his involvement with start-ups, Schlichting worked in mergers and acquisitions for Morgan Stanley & Co. and then with William E. Simon making private equity investments.

In addition, colleagues at Zone Ventures (the Los Angeles satellite of Draper, Fisher, Jurvetson, a major Silicon Valley venture capital firm) introduced them to the first CTO that they had ever been truly thrilled with. And they found another business development person at an industry conference. With the basic crew in place, both cofounders try to spend about 20 percent of their time recruiting. Luckily, they've found that all good hires seem to bring at least one excellent person along with them.

They try to choose employees with whom they have "chemistry" and who express excitement about the idea behind HIWIRE. Then, to keep people motivated, they keep employee options "topped up." This means that along with bonuses, the company makes sure that employees continue to have a sufficient number of outstanding, unvested options so that their current positions will be on par with any outside offers, and so that the latter will be less likely to be a distraction. Pavilak and Lambert say it is helpful that the company is still small and in its early stages, because everyone involved is still strongly motivated by the opportunity.

The company's primary source of revenue is the targeting and distribution of in-stream audio advertisements for both traditional and online radio stations. Its goal is to allow streaming content producers to derive revenue from their listeners no matter where those listeners are physically located. Right now, each additional listener to a radio station costs the station about ten cents an hour, and there is no model in place to recover its costs outside its local area. Radio stations make most of their money by selling local ads. National ads sell for a much lower rate and represent only a fraction of revenue. HIWIRE gives stations the ability to turn all ads into high-value local ads.

The reason HIWIRE has chosen this revenue model is that its founders believe that the most exciting future stream of revenues for online radio stations will come from inserting local ads for listeners who are far from the original broadcasting location. By using anonymous data collected by the HIWIRE tuner—much as the cable television industry does now—the company has positioned itself to provide this ad insertion service on the basis of its audience measurements.

However, Pavilak is careful to note, "Right now, even revenues are not that important." He says that now is the time of the land grab and that market position is most highly valued at this point. At this stage of the game, Internet companies are valued on their partnerships and their distribution—not on profitability.

As previously mentioned, HIWIRE has great success in signing significant deals with distribution partners. The first of these was MusicMatch, a popular MP3 player that gets between 30,000 and 45,000 downloads a day and has more than two million regular users. The HIWIRE tuner is integrated with the MP3 player that MusicMatch released in November 1999. Because the MusicMatch user base is extremely loyal and enthusiastic about downloading new versions of the player, the Rocket tuner as an integrated component of the MP3 player went out to over 90 percent of existing MusicMatch users. By the end of the year 2000, the integrated Rocket tuner/MusicMatch MP3 player should be an icon on a minimum of one million Dell PCs and between one and two and a half million Hewlett-Packard PCs.

HIWIRE also has a contract with College-broadcast. com, a media and entertainment aggregator with access to 15 million college students. It also has a number of signed letters of intent with various ISPs and popular Web sites. Partnerships such as these are anticipated to not only help the company achieve distribution that will exceed that gained by the most aggressive marketing programs, but also help to significantly strengthen its partners' positions.

Right now, while there are several software applications and Web sites that offer audio and video entertainment, there is no other online radio tuner company pursuing the same business strategy for entering into distribution and content partnerships as HIWIRE. Thus, the company believes it has a significant headstart in these areas and, as a result, is well positioned to achieve a first-mover advantage in streaming ad targeting and insertion.

Pavilak says that distinctions between the different players in the audio space are important for understanding the industry. The first and most obvious distinction is the difference between streaming media and specific files that are downloaded and saved on a user's hard drive before being watched or heard. MP3 files, for example, are downloaded and saved before being opened. Radio or TV programs, in contrast, are streamed in real-time as the user listens and watches.

The second distinction has to do with tuners, or players, that direct or connect users to actual radio stations. Players in the latter category include Spinner, Net Radio, and Imagine Radio, which play preprogrammed channels of commercial-free music and are commonly referred to as jukeboxes. Rocket is not grouped with these products because it points to actual radio and television stations that broadcast over the Web (including online-only stations).

The third distinction has to do with Web–based applications versus those that reside on the desktop. Web site–based applications, called aggregators, link to online radio stations and stream content through their sites out to users. Companies in this category include Broadcast.com, BRS, WebRadio, and Kerbango. HIWIRE's difference from this group is that its tuner resides as a separate application on the user's desktop. Pavilak believes that as a result, HIWIRE provides listeners with "an easier, more user-friendly way to listen to online radio." In fact, many of the features that HIWIRE promotes are in direct response to so-called aggregators, whose response times and navigation can be slow. In addition, because it is a stand-alone application, the HIWIRE platform is free from the vagaries of the browser environment. Finally, unlike Web-based applications, its tuner provides both its own company and its partners with desktop branding.

The final distinction involves business strategies. Microsoft, RealNetworks, QuickTime, and WebRadio—the four most commonly heard names in this sector—all have tuner-like devices that they give away in an effort to increase the demand for their proprietary software. They distribute tuners solely as a means to increase sales of their server software. RealNetworks currently claims to have an 85 percent share of the aggregator market and touts 79 million registered downloaded copies of its Real-Player. However, it is being challenged by Microsoft in a bitter battle because Microsoft is giving away free streaming server software in an attempt to gain market share in the server software market. Either Microsoft or RealNetworks would offer a considerable competitive threat if it decided to pursue HIWIRE's market, but HIWIRE has the advantage of being "code agnostic," meaning it will accept audio streams in either the Windows Media Player or RealNetworks RealPlayer format. This feature will gain importance if Microsoft, RealNetworks, or any other competitor starts to develop significant market share.

### Approach to Personnel Management

HIWIRE chooses employees with whom it has "chemistry" and who express excitement about the industry it's in. To motivate people, it keeps employee options "topped up"—the company makes sure that employees continue to have a number of outstanding, unvested options so that their current positions will be on par with any outside offers.

## FUTURE PLANS

HIWIRE does significant market research for its business. Its employees scour Web and technology publications for trends it will need to consider for the future. It also listens carefully to its partners and customers—those who create online content as well as traditional radio programmers—about what they think listeners are looking for. Employees also read every bit of feedback that comes from the HIWIRE site.

"Customer feedback is the basis of all Internet business," opines Pavilak. "The Internet is a network of services, and as soon as one of these services is launched, it must be instantly ready to evolve." HIWIRE actively solicits feedback with a button on its site, which takes a user to the menu listing various aspects of its product that they can comment on. Because the company considers user feedback to be vitally important, "even the harshest criticism is welcome," Pavilak says.

Another important aspect of planning for the future is keeping up with changing technologies, which is a major challenge in the Internet and computer industry. Employees keep in touch with industry analysts and consultants as much as they can. Publications they follow include *The Industry Standard, FastCompany, Radio Ink, Radio and Records, Wired, Internet Weekly, The New York Times,* and *The Wall Street Journal.* Online lists on streaming media include WebNoize and the Streaming Media Newsletter.

One definite interest of HIWIRE for the future is to develop markets beyond U.S. borders. To this end, it has distribution agreements that will help place its software on the desktops of millions of computers in Asia and in Europe over the next few years. The company is also creating localized language versions of its tuner and developing relationships with international station groups.

"Oddly enough," says Pavilak, "the first foreign language version that we are delivering is in Chinese. While there are precious few Internet-connected computers in China right now, it is clear that there is fantastic potential there. Internet usage by the world Chinese expatriate population is significant. Chinese language ISPs such as SINA.net claim millions of users all over the world." Once the Chinese version is completed, French, Italian, German, and Spanish versions will follow.

"It's surprising how many of us U.S.-based Internet businesses seem to forget to pay attention to markets beyond our borders," says Pavilak. "Data point: A couple of years ago the international market for U.S.-made movies surpassed the U.S. market for the same movies. It's some real business."

Luckily, HIWIRE thinks it has a competitive advantage as it looks forward. According to Pavilak, widespread Internet adoption, the ubiquitousness of multimedia PCs, and the evolution of media streaming technologies have paved the way for a new generation of entertainment: online broadcasting. In late 1997, when the company first developed its idea for an online tuner, Internet radio was virtually nonexistent. Since then, more than 2000 stations have begun broadcasting their signals online, and the radio industry is beginning to recognize the opportunities presented by the Internet strategies. During that same time period, approximately 29 percent of Americans with access to the Internet have listened to online radio at least once. This number continues to climb rapidly as more people gain access to the Internet and its broad offerings of online radio stations from around the world.

Also, the fundamentals of the radio industry have changed little over the past fifty years and remain strong. Since the introduction of FM radio in the 1940s, demand has stayed consistent, and an estimated 95 percent of all teenagers and adults listen to an average of twenty-two hours of radio per week, according to statistics kept by Arbitron. In the United States, the number of radio stations has grown annually at a rate of less than 3 percent since 1970 and now hovers around 13,000. Strict Federal Communications Commission (FCC) regulations of signal strength, as well as significant equipment costs, have limited stations to highly competitive local markets.

Thus stations must battle for local listeners, as well as face ever-increasing competition from new stations and emerging nontraditional digital, satellite, and cable broadcasters. Online broadcasting (or Webcasting), in contrast, has gained popularity quickly with both broadcasters and listeners over the past couple of years. The number of stations that Webcast has grown from practically none in 1997 to over 2700 stations today. This adoption rate is far faster than that experienced by any other audio technology, including AM and FM radio, cassettes, and even CDs.

Furthermore, also according to Arbitron, one out of four traditional listeners tune into online radio because they are dissatisfied with local content for reasons ranging from not being able to find music they like to wanting better news and information. Unrestricted by geography or regulation, online radio enables such listeners to receive nonlocal content covering a broad range of interests and events—morning talk shows, concerts, interviews, sports events, and niche music styles.

But while traditional (i.e., terrestrial) stations are eager to enjoy the benefits of online broadcasting, they struggle with how to pay for high volumes of Web traffic. There is currently no means to capture online broadcast advertising revenues because at this stage, no equivalent to the Arbitron survey exists for quantifying and profiling online listeners. Once a station's signal is broadcast over the Internet, only national ads have any relevance for listeners outside a station's traditional terrestrial broadcast listening area. As a result, Webcasting currently functions primarily to promote brand loyalty by increasing click-throughs on station Web sites.

Here, again, is where HIWIRE comes in, and where it thinks it has well positioned itself for the future. It is banking on the belief that an enormous opportunity exists for companies that can provide solutions that allow stations and advertisers to unlock the targeted advertising potential of online broadcasting.

### Vision of the New Economy

The major sources of revenue on the Internet are simply unimagined at this point, and they will come about when the Internet is disconnected from desktop computers and the connection is instead "everywhere and in everything." Companies will be able to reach their audiences based on location or any other demographic information with advertisements that are targeted and inserted into whatever content users happen to be tapped into: audio if they are listening, video if they are watching, or something noninvasive if they are reading online. The companies that will set themselves apart are those building themselves with great technology and a keen eye for utility and long-term growth and make their value proposition very clear.

## HIWIRE RECOMMENDS . . .

Like so many other Internet entrepreneurs, Jim Pavilak believes the most important piece of advice he was given when starting his business was to stick with the vision and have the courage to follow it through. "Tenacity," he says, "is an incredibly important resource."

This is especially so in the case of the Internet, where everything is being created from scratch. Pavilak and Lambert, for example, found that building a piece of software for the Internet is entirely different than building one-to-one software. "You need an extra year to build a robust and scalable system that can handle millions of users," says Pavilak. Even though people are enthusiastic about the concept of streaming media and willing to put up with some inconsistencies in the beginning, inevitably they dislike broken connections, erratic service, and software glitches on the tuners. Thus, there's constant hard work given to improving the system.

The results of tenacity at HIWIRE have been gratifying, however. "People seem to like choices and variety, [which we are able to offer]," says Pavilak. If a baseball game isn't available on the radio at work, for example, but it is being broadcast to a tiny AM station that streams to the Internet, a person can launch the HIWIRE tuner and then listen to the game that way. "Since our main purpose is to provide a way for stations to pay for their Internet broadcasts through audio ads, those stations like our product because it helps them to show that critical revenue stream we all must tap into or perish."

Something else Pavilak finds gratifying is being able to take a concept, disassemble it into tasks for separate departments, and then reassemble all the components so that they come back into a real product. The payoff from the hard work is actually seeing it all work together.

He and Lambert also note that there are some legal issues that anyone developing an Internet start-up should be aware of. Taking their first outside investment required a surprising amount of time, attention, legal documentation, and cost. The paperwork for the company's first angel round was almost fifty pages thick. ("One of our angels was just getting started and quite a stickler, and, surprisingly, the lawyers on our side didn't seem to have experience preparing this form, either," says Pavilak.) HIWIRE spent almost 15 percent of the angel round just on legal fees.

In retrospect, Pavilak believes that you should be able to say with absolute confidence to your investors that the angel term sheet (investor terms) does not have to be any more than three pages long—"especially considering that it will be completely torn up if you are successful enough to attract a first venture capital round. It's the standard formula: When the VCs come in, they negotiate a completely new term sheet."

If you do not succeed in attracting a first round, the angel investors will probably just lose their money anyway, he says. "They know that you and your idea are a big gamble with a huge payoff. It's pretty much all or nothing. Good tech angels are the real gunslingers of our time. They go with their guts, act quickly, and take their chances. It sounds too obvious, but there are so many new angel investors out there that you may wind up accepting money from someone who isn't experienced with the way the deal works yet."

Once you've dealt with the legal issues surrounding getting financing, there are still plenty of new ones that crop up, says Pavilak. "Once we [HIWIRE] started picking up momentum and signed on with a law firm with strong tech deal experience, we found ourselves buried in all manner of financial documents, deal memos, and letters of intent. All of these have been turned into solid working contracts. And while we were delighted to be in this predicament, crafting and completing all these documents is time-consuming and requires an awful lot of precious thought."

Since you are also busy creating a new business, he adds, "you'll want to make sure to spare a few brainwaves so you can think creatively about where your most potent opportunity is and how you are going to go about creating your market." And since the Internet business moves and changes at an unprecedented speed, it's important to continue moving your company forward and getting all of your deals done before they go out of date.

HIWIRE recommends aligning yourself with strong lawyers that know the territory. Hopefully, at least some of them will be interested in and engaged by your business. One of HIWIRE's first hires was its vice president of business development, a transactional lawyer who is passionate about the business and extremely capable of whipping up good first draft agreements. He is someone who can get drafts done in "Internet time" and then send them off to real lawyers to have them completed.

Interestingly, Pavilak says that at first his company had great partners at the large and well-respected Internet law firms, but that over time, one by one, they left to join Internet start-ups. Once these early contacts within the firms had left, the turnaround time for deals increased significantly, so HIWIRE brought on a small army of legal advisers. It enlisted the help of an additional IP firm, beefed up with two more legal consultants, and recently retained an experienced in-house counselor.

Finally, like so many of the other companies featured in this book, Pavilak thinks that having a reliable advisory board is absolutely critical to the success of an Internet start-up. "We're blessed with a fantastic advisory board," he says. "They keep us on track with valuable advice that helps hone our mission and our products. They are a constant source of ideas and inspiration, not to mention contacts. Spend the time and energy to seek out those people you respect the most in your industry and do whatever it takes to get them involved with your company," he advises.

HIWIRE's advisory board includes individuals with experience in areas such as investment banking (Robert Emery, president of BankBoston Robertson Stephens); interactive marketing (Bruce Judson, founder and editor of *Bruce Judson's Grow Your Profits*); enhanced TV (Randy Komisar, chairman of IQ Commerce); human-centered design (Dr. Don Norman, president of Unext Learning Systems); and strategic consulting (Rob Shurtleff, founder of S.L. Partners). Their collective experience includes work with such high-profile Internet and technology companies as WebMD, Open Market, Inc., TiVo, and WebTV, among many others. A stellar advisory board can easily open doors for a start-up on the basis of their experience and connections alone.

## A LOVE OF THE INTERNET

Pavilak calls himself "one of those digital junkies." The Internet is "how I keep a sense of the pulse and condition of the world," he says, as well as keep in touch with most of his friends and business associates. He e-mails, reads news and humor, tracks stocks, and enjoys "listening to fantastic radio programs from all over the place," all on-line.

When asked what his company can do through the Internet that it couldn't do through traditional means, his answer is simple: "Exist. What we are doing here could not be done at all by traditional means. In our case, the Internet has suddenly—in a historical sense, with due credit to the people who worked a long time to build the Internet—caused an immense expansion of the broadcast area for radio stations. There we were, with ten to twenty stations on the FM dial, for instance, complaining that they were all controlled by two or three giant conglomerates or some political party [in the case of a PBS], and then wham! A person can have a phone line put in, buy a server, and broadcast to the entire planet. This is a big deal in every sense of the term."

"Everyone has heard of the squabbles between the pirate stations and the FCC," he says. "Well, for about the same price of buying a transmitter to cover a couple of square miles, the pirate station can just forget about the FCC and go online. The frontier is vast and undeveloped; our job is to build the infrastructure. We can start from scratch and do right when all we could have done before was complain or make do."

"I've often been reminded of a forest I saw in South Florida about two months after a big hurricane passed through," he explains. "The hurricane completely leveled all the plants; even the biggest trees were snapped off about three feet above the ground. Within the time between the hurricane and my visit, every living plant had been growing and fruiting at about 400 percent of its normal activity. It was a very basic attempt to take maximum advantage of a 'new' environment. The plants that could distribute their offspring in the most efficient manner were going to have the largest share of the forest terrain. What an excellent analogy for the Internet! We're laying down the infrastructure on a new and previously uninhabited planet."

Or to describe it another way, he says, "Deep at the bottom of the ocean there are thermal vents spewing forth incredibly hot water. For a long time, it was thought that nothing could live in these environments. Now we've discovered that they are teeming with life. It is thought that all life on the planet may have come from such places. The Internet is like that—superheated, full of new life. It's the most exciting place to be right now."

The major sources of revenue on the Internet are simply unimagined at this point, and they will come about when the Internet is disconnected from desktop computers and the connection to it, in Pavilak's words, "is everywhere and in everything . . . [in effect] when the Internet becomes like electricity."

He says that even before then, advertising buys will stop being tied to content, a development HIWIRE is already taking advantage of. Companies will soon be able to reach their audiences based on location or any other demographic information with advertisements that are targeted and inserted into whatever content users happen to be tapped into. Also, he says that these ads will be more appropriate to the aspect of the Internet the user is experiencing: audio if you are listening, video if you are watching ad banners, or something noninvasive and new if you are reading.

Not surprisingly, Pavilak thinks that running an Internet business is completely different from running a traditional brick-and-mortar business: "On the Internet you are competing with every brain on earth—in real time! Ever try registering a wacky but brilliant domain name that you just made up? It's taken!''

Each and every day, he spends hours worrying about every little detail his company has to negotiate: "Ten to twelve hours of creative strategizing and plotting the future. Four to six hours of sleep, during which you dream about having an octopus-like pet that is fascinating but dangerous," he says, only half-joking. "One to three hours of some sort of physical exertion, which will hopefully result in a temporary state of mental cleanliness. No, the math doesn't work if you add up the hours: That's the way it is."

Other challenges in running an Internet start-up include the need for capital and "finding the balance between patience and passion that you'll need to survive this process." As for the funding challenge, "It's binary; you either get funded or you don't. The whole time you are out there, dying to get into the race, meeting with potential investors and pitching yourself and your big idea, you don't get to know how close or far you are from getting the start you need. You can be out there full-time for months and not know if you are days away from having to take a job somewhere or a day away from a term sheet. In the meantime, you actively scan the horizon for signs that one of the established players is making an announcement that they are replicating your dream or that some small group of smart businesspeople and engineers has popped up out of nowhere and is doing the same." Exciting but scary.

Then, after you've gotten your idea off the ground, Pavilak says you need to move quickly to build a company that can be a real competitor online. Then the challenge becomes delegation. You need to have the confidence to turn over responsibility; that is the only way to grow. You need to build a team that can deal with any obstacle or opportunity that may present itself.

One positive byproduct, of course, is that employees are more likely to feel that they are making a genuine impact on the business when they are working at an Internet company. "Making a great deal or putting together a partnership is satisfying," says Pavilak. "Even more satisfying is watching a handpicked group of individuals respond to a crisis and completely manage or even profit from it in some way."

In his opinion, the Internet companies that are approaching the new landscape best are those that are building themselves with great technology and a keen eye for utility and long-term growth. The ones that are making mistakes are those that are not innovative enough. "Many of them seem to be doing exactly the same thing," he says. "For example, is there any new company out there that does not claim that it will make billions selling CDs through its hip new music portal catering to eighteen- to twenty-four-year-olds? I think you can buy a CD from about 800 million sites today."

Other strategies he dislikes? "[Companies that resort] to the use of sophomoric copy in ads [and] pretend to be iconoclasts because they just do not have a convincing business model. I often wonder which Internet start-up will be the first on network television to use the full range of sounds producible by every human body orifice."

Online businesses Pavilak actually likes and uses include Mapquest, when he's on trips, and Hotmail, because "from time to time I can't easily get to my computer." But the Web site where he actually spends cash money most often is Southwest's. "They make it a reasonable proposition for a customer to arrange a flight. Southwest has a simple proposition—buy online for double frequent flyer miles—and then makes it simple to follow through." In Pavilak's opinion, sites that sell services need to make their value proposition crystal clear and "are crazy to put up any additional and clearly unnecessary barriers for customers, such as special access codes that must be memorized or saved in a safe place. Southwest gets by fine without the additional barriers," he notes, and as a result, he's purchased dozens of flights from its Web site. It can be challenging enough for some customers to get on to the Web in the first place, not to mention find the site you're looking for and then do something with it.

To take advantage of that wonderful new medium called the Internet, HIWIRE is concentrating on doing just that: making its value proposition clear—and gaining customers. "No crazes last, but the profound changes that the Internet brings will endure," says Pavilak. "When the hype and craze of the Internet cool down, naturally it will become much more important for a company to be profitable. Until then, it'll still be all about gaining market share."

# 11

# The Keys to Success in the Future of the Internet

*Those entrepreneurs who are the first to harness the still rapidly developing capabilities of the Internet will become the new market leaders of the Internet revolution*

Because the Internet is changing so rapidly, many of the keys to success are different from what they may have been even months before. Different business models will go in and out of favor, and new technologies will appear and create a need for complementary products and services. There are, however, certain key aspects that will, for the most part, forever hold true. The role of the entrepreneur, manager, investor, or employee is to keep on top of these developments and find ways to capitalize on your particular knowledge of an industry, product, service, or technology to maximize the return on your investment.

## MODELS FOR SUCCESS

The most ironic part is that when you talk to almost every Internet entrepreneur who has successfully "made it," there was often a time in his or her career when failure seemed to loom ahead. Every Internet company encounters numerous setbacks and obstacles along every stage of its development. The perfect case in point is America Online, which only a few short years ago was widely vilified and disparaged as having low-class technology and, according to the conventional wisdom at the time, was bound to be eaten alive by Microsoft Corp. What a difference five years can make. Today, a lot of people wish they had invested in AOL even two years. There is no prescribed model for success with Internet companies— whether an entrepreneur, CEO, or employee, you should look to continually challenge the norm and look for innovative ways to grow.

## WHERE ELSE TO LOOK FOR SUCCESSFUL BUSINESS MODELS?

The Internet is transforming the entire world economy, and its impact will only increase. With the Internet turning so many industries on their heads, there exist count-less opportunities to capitalize on it at some level. How? Study what is happening in the markets. Look where venture capitalists are investing their money. Follow the comments of the leaders of Internet companies and where they say the industry is going. And most important, for-mulate your own thoughts, for that is the true way to beat the masses and get in on the ground floor. The key is hav-ing the resources to properly exploit opportunities once you find them. There are a million good ideas out there, yet 99 percent of those people who fail never make it be-cause of failed execution.

*Industry Research*

It is becoming increasingly difficult to stay on top of all the developments, and their implications, occurring in the Internet industry. Nevertheless, the Internet itself makes it possible to receive a steady stream of news bytes on various subjects, all in an e-mail delivered right to your desktop. Because the Internet allows for such easy customization of information directly to you, it is simply a matter of finding the right news engine that will provide you with the information you need. Sites such as Yahoo!, Netscape, and Excite allow you to customize their page so that you receive specific news of interest. Online publi-cations such as *The Red Herring* and *Internet World News* provide brief stories every day on Internet and technol-ogy-related happenings, particularly news related to the many partnerships and alliances companies are pursuing to secure a foothold in the online world. Most avid In-ternet enthusiasts end up subscribing to a number of these sources and quickly peruse them each day for information on what's relevant to their own lines of business or may potentially impact them in some way.

Even with the customization functionality of many Internet news engines, it is still extremely difficult to keep up to date with and digest everything that is happening. One reason is that there are now so many Internet companies that most of the small ones receive very little press, even though it's these small companies that frequently build or generate a new technology, product, or service that will have a serious effect on a market. Entrepreneurs should be reading a whole slew of industry magazines, such as *The Industry Standard* and *Wired*, and even more general financial publications, such as *The Wall Street Journal, FastCompany,* and *BusinessWeek*. In addition, there are many new publications—*Silicon Alley Reporter, Alley Cat News, Digital Coast Weekly, Tech Capital, Internet World*—and other regional publications that cover breaking news in hotbed areas of Internet growth. These are great sources for tracking those smaller companies that may not yet have surfaced in the major publications.

Equally important is to keep learning about the new Web-based applications that are emerging. Spend time with people—programmers, venture capitalists, research analysts, consultants, and other entrepreneurs—who know a particular industry or product or service well, and share ideas with them. This is often where new ideas come from or where you are able to fine-tune an existing idea. Also spend time with industry veterans; pick their brains about the past and what they anticipate the future holds for their particular industry.

## BUILD THE IDEA

The idea is the easy part. There are millions of ideas out there waiting to be capitalized on. Successful entrepreneurs are the ones who know how to turn an idea into a reality—quickly, because in the Internet era, new businesses are started ever second. Once you have the idea, it is a race against everyone else out there to develop it into a profitable business. Because so many Internet-based businesses have such low barriers to entry, it opens the playing field to a wave of new competition. The key is having some comparative advantage, be it a member of your management team, a patented technology, a strategic alliance, or some other weapon that gives you an added edge.

Furthermore, every good business idea is in a constant state of development. There are always new components of the idea developing with the business heading in new directions. In order to keep moving continuously forward, businesses must always be thinking of new ideas, new applications, or complementary products and services that can make the business stronger, more diverse, and ready to take the next step. Every achievement your business makes—whether a specific sales goal, an important alliance, or a new product or service—should be leveraged into something even greater. Keep setting the goals a notch higher; this is how you build a valuable company. Don't fall into the trap of spending time thinking about how great you are doing; think of new ways to do even better. So much can be gained or lost in Internet time. Every business is now vulnerable to competition. Once you have your idea, go with it.

## WRITE THE BUSINESS PLAN

The business plan is an integral part of developing an Internet company. Business plans tend to change constantly, especially in a rapidly developing space such as the Internet. Those companies that are able to develop a business plan that allows them to update their business model with new technologies, products, and services will be well positioned for the twenty-first century. The business plan should serve as your guide to your business, regardless of whether you are just starting a company or have been in business for years.

Your plan can be a twenty-page PowerPoint presentation or a fifty-page document, whatever you are most comfortable with. If you are just starting a business, it is a good idea to keep the plan concise, especially if you are using it as a tool to solicit investors. In reality, the potential investor (especially if it is a venture capitalist) is probably only going to read a paragraph or two of the executive summary before deciding whether it is worth reading any further.

The business plan is a document that should also be updated on a consistent basis. Even if your business is already up on its feet, devote time on a quarterly or semi-annual basis to updating your business plan. This effort forces you to take a step back and analyze where the business is and what you need to change for the future. A business plan forces you to develop your thoughts on every level and defend them to the reader. Encourage your advisers and management team to give their comments. This is often the best way to fine-tune existing strategies and come up with new ideas. The key is making sure that the business model you develop in your business plan can thrive in a marketplace that is in a continuous state of change.

## EXECUTE, EXECUTE, EXECUTE

Generating the business idea and even documenting it in a business plan is, again, the easy part—the implementation is what makes or breaks the opportunity. Internet entrepreneurs are known for their lofty ideas (and valuation notions regarding their own companies). Yet the most successful ones are those that spend less time talking and more time assembling the right team to capitalize on the opportunity. It is impossible for any one person to truly capitalize on an idea fully. Once you have an idea, there are usually so many things that need to be done that the best way to cover all of the areas is to build a team to help you. The key is to recruit individuals who have better skills than you do in a particular area and who share your vision for the company and your drive to succeed. Remember, as soon as you have an idea, the race is on to see how quickly you can develop it and beat any potential competitors to the marketplace with a superior product or service.

## GROW YOUR TALENT POOL

Internet entrepreneurs are notorious for having to wear many hats. From CEO to recruiter to fact-checker, Internet entrepreneurs must do it all. This trend has had an impact on employees at every level. You are much less apt to hear an employee at an Internet company say, "That's not my job." Granted, most Internet companies start out smaller; however, the "do everything" mentality that is with them from the beginning often sticks and makes its way throughout the ranks in the company. Individuals realize that when the CEO is making his or her own copies, they can perform the more mundane tasks as well. There are very few secretaries anymore; they are assistants—individuals who help on specific projects, gather information, or perform more "real work." There is no room in an Internet company for someone who cannot at least try to wear different hats. You'll find that it is vital to be able to mobilize your resources to move in a different direction on a second's notice. One of the biggest challenges for Internet companies is finding smart, eager-to-learn, and motivated employees who can roll with the punches as the company grows.

*The Business Team*

The business team is the most important part of your venture. Regardless of how good your idea is, it will never succeed without the right partners. Every employee is a critical hire. As your business grows, it becomes harder to put each potential employee under your personal microscope; however, if you hire the right people along the way and instill in them the right company values, they should be able to do it for you. No company, regardless of size, can afford a bad hire—and there is no reason to. Take your time in building your team, because it is a difficult decision to undo once you have hired someone.

Teamwork becomes even more important if your Internet start-up is understaffed (as is frequently the case). Then employees are overworked and still expected to compete and win against much larger, more established competitors. The key to success, then, often is simply working more efficiently as a team. The more your employees understand about different areas of the company, the more they will be able to contribute to the business as a whole. Encourage everyone to work together in some way or another. Institute employee focus groups to address certain issues, or just encourage employees to become "visitors" in other groups for a week.

### Employees as Owners

Make every employee in your new venture an owner. From the receptionists to the management team, give them the opportunity to own some level of the company. This creates lasting ties to the business and immediately creates a different mindset for your employees. Everyone has heard stories about Internet companies and the effect stock options have had on even the most junior employee. Give your employees that hope—make them owners. It will be one of the best executive decisions you ever make.

## OFFICE ENVIRONMENT

Another way to cater to your in-house talent is to create the best office environment possible. Do everything you can to promote happy employees, because this effort will pay for itself tenfold over time. Take people around and introduce them to everyone and explain what they will be doing. One Internet company, The Motley Fool, has pizza every other Friday for its employees and a birthday event once a month for all employees whose birthdays fall in that month. It also routinely sends around a survey to find out how it can be making its employees happier. Not surprisingly, The Motley Fool has been voted one of the best Internet companies to work at.

In the workplace, make everyone feel important and treat people at every level with respect. Once a quarter, do something to surprise your employees. Whether it is a bonus, an impromptu party, or a special event—your efforts will make your employees feel appreciated. This is how you build a happy team, and a happy team is more likely to work harder and believe in the company.

## BRAINSTORM

Too many companies lose employees to new start-up ventures because they did not give them the outlet to voice their ideas. Employees at all levels deal with customers, suppliers, competitors, and other individuals who provide valuable feedback that can often lead to new ways to conduct business. Harness these ideas in-house before one of your star employees becomes your competitor.

Conduct brainstorming sessions once a month. Keep the groups to ten people or less, preferably from different areas of the company, and encourage every person, regardless of title, to come up with as many ideas as possible on new products and services your company could be offering. Make it an informal gathering, and try and get everyone's creative juices flowing by playing music, serving pizza, or having a cocktail. You will be surprised at the number of people who actually come to the brainstorming sessions with ideas already. Another suggestion from Internet entrepreneurs is to avoid setting up offices with doors where there is no interaction; make your office space as open as possible in order to encourage the uninhibited flow of ideas. By putting everyone together to brainstorm ideas, it will enable ideas to grow and change based on the input of new individuals.

## ATTITUDE

The bottom line is to create an environment that fosters a positive attitude in as many ways as possible. Attitude is so important, regardless of your profession or industry. The speed at which business is conducted over the Internet is unlike anything most of us have ever been a part of. It is imperative to learn how to act decisively and alter your business model on a second's notice. A record number of partnerships, joint ventures, mergers, and acquisitions happen every moment, continually altering the landscape of every industry. Your ability to react to these events and align the attitudes of your team is crucial. Being part of an Internet company usually means putting an overwhelming amount of faith in the management team (and many late nights). You must be able to instill in your team a sense of unity and belief in what you are doing, at all times.

## VC MANIA

Venture capitalists have always been a good barometer of market activity. There have never been so many investments made as there have been in the Internet and technology industry over the past few years. Whereas venture capitalists usually wait anywhere from five to seven years

for a return on their invested capital, they have been
known to make ten times their money in a matter of
months with an investment in an Internet start-up. As
VCs keeping making more money from these deals, investors want to put in even more money, and they seek new
deals to invest in.

In truth, probably only three out of ten Internet companies will make it, yet that is enough to potentially double or even triple the return on investments made into a
VC fund. Whereas venture capitalists historically have
not focused their investment dollars in start-up opportunities, there is now so much competition among VCs to
get in on good deals that they are forced to look at start-
ups. Not that this is a bad thing. Getting in on the ground
floor and at the lowest valuation possible can make the
best returns, but it is also true that there is more money
than there are good business opportunities right now.

Who are these VCs and where did they come from?
Venture capitalists have been around for a long time.
They have been thrust into the spotlight because of the
mind-boggling returns on many of their investments. VC
firms tend to be small, employing anywhere from two to
twenty individuals; however, the better ones are among
the most profitable businesses in the world. New venture
capital firms are starting everywhere, just waiting for the
chance to invest in the next eBay or Yahoo! As competition among VC firms has increased, more and more companies are getting funded. But that doesn't mean that it
is easy for just anyone to get funded.

VCs always emphasize the management team's experience and its competitive advantage in the marketplace.
Once they are sold on these aspects of a company, the investment decision gets down to the topic of valuation.

Valuing a business, especially for early-stage Internet companies, is more an art than a science—and each VC firm has its own valuation methods. Established investment groups, such as the Harvard Endowment Fund and numerous pension funds, are big investors in VC funds. The VCs, once called "vulture capitalists," are now thought to be some of the most savvy business people in the marketplace. Their connections and deep pockets make them an excellent resource for any Internet company at any level.

## CHOOSE YOUR INVESTORS WISELY

Many entrepreneurs often mistakenly take the first source of capital that comes their way. Investors should bring more to the table than just money. Good investors should also be business partners and play a somewhat active role in opening doors for your business.

Although the first topic of discussion with investors is inevitably valuation—how much is your company currently worth?—there will always be discrepancies on how to value Internet start-ups especially. Our advice to you is to be realistic about the valuation for your business. Remember that although the amount of capital the VC wishes to invest is important, just as important are the other intangibles it will bring to the table. For example, venture capitalists are often great business partners because of their network of contacts and investments in other companies. Venture capitalists oftentimes try to form their own *keiretsus* (discussed later in this chapter) where they promote partnerships and frequently mergers and acquisitions among their portfolio companies.

For start-ups, another popular source of financing comes from angels. Angel investors are often high net-worth individuals who invest in start-up opportunities and oftentimes have a more hands-off approach than venture capitalists (though rarely are VCs ever involved in the daily operations of the company, either). Regardless of how your company is financed, it is important that your investors are active on some level with your company. Your investors are another validation for your company, so it is important that you can speak outwardly about your investors and why they invested in your company.

## Find a Good Lawyer

Many entrepreneurs undervalue the importance of having capable legal representation. Although lawyers are often a "secondary expense" when starting a business, it is extremely important to pick the right legal counsel from the start. Remember that lawyers in general bill by the hour. Therefore, you can choose to handle limited legal work at the start when your funds are tight. The key is having them there from the start for when particular situations arise.

A good lawyer is someone you want to feel comfortable with and who, importantly, understands your industry. There are thousands of law firms, ranging from extremely large to one-person firms; however, a law firm is only as good as the attorney(s) you are working with. Also remember that lawyers are not general business advisers (although many would like to think they are). Keep them focused on the legal matters, not general business issues. The Internet has created a whole new type of "legal headache" for everyone from lawyers to entrepreneurs to established companies. Find a lawyer who understands your business and can dedicate the necessary time for you today and in the future.

## SET GOALS

Every company should have goals. Without them, there is no way for you or your employees to push themselves to get that extra piece of business or to have a sense of accomplishment from reaching a specific milestone. Every employee should have their own short (one month), medium (six months), and long-term (one year) goals for the company. Remember, ten times as much can happen in Internet time than in the past. Therefore, it is extremely important to be frequently revisiting these goals and updating them based on new developments within the business. Goals are the way to grow your business. Keep pushing them outward and striving for new successes. The opportunities capitalized on to reach a certain milestone can usually be leveraged into even greater opportunities in the future.

## LEVERAGE YOUR CONTACTS

You can never have enough contacts. Regardless of whether they are in the Internet industry or not, the more contacts you have the better. Find a way to keep in touch with these people. A personal e-mail once every couple of months or a breakfast meeting is more than enough to keep a lasting relationship.

The Internet industry is the perfect example of the power of contacts. Believe it or not, even with the incredible number of Internet companies already developed, there are only a few distinct inner circles of leading players. Venture capitalists, investment bankers, and public Internet company CEOs are the most likely to be admitted to this inner circle. In fact, venture capitalists especially try to create their own inner circles of companies they have funded in order to promote partnerships and the growth of these companies. This will change and new circles of industry leaders and innovators will develop; however, it still pays to meet as many players as possible. You never know when one of these individuals is going to "hit jackpot" with their company and be immediately vaulted into the ranks of the "Internet revolutionaries."

## EFFECTIVELY UTILIZE YOUR ADVISERS

Advisers are another extremely important part of every company. Do not run out and ask your father or best friend to be on your advisory board. Look for established industry veterans who will be able to open doors for you and who have an interest in your business. Industry leaders, venture capitalists, investment bankers, lawyers, and consultants can make excellent advisers. Make your dream list of potential advisers and then find a way to get them interested. Whether through a referral or even a cold call, you have to sell them on your idea. Many will already be on numerous other advisory boards and may have little time for "just another Internet idea." Sell yourself, your business, and why you are going to succeed. Give them a vested interest in your business. Usually, you cannot afford to pay these individuals enough to make it worth their while; however, by giving them some level of equity compensation you can attract them.

The bottom line is that advisers need to have a vested interest in the business if you expect to get the most out of them. Be ready to be "grilled" on your business model, financials, and everything else. Good advisers will force you to answer the difficult questions to them, instead of to investors and customers. A strong advisory board also lends credibility to your business. This can be crucial when landing investments and the first wave of customers.

## PLAN AHEAD

Internet revolutionaries are consistently ten steps ahead of their competitors. They are constantly looking into the future to understand how their company can be better positioned to take advantage of future opportunities. Time spent on what happened in the past is wasted time. To be sure, there are things to be learned from previous courses of action; however, the majority of your time should be spent preparing for the future. The greatest entrepreneurs of our time all have faced adversity of some sort, as will every entrepreneur blazing a new trail instead of following in the trail of others. But those who plan ahead are the most prepared to capitalize on the opportunities of tomorrow. This means encouraging employees to pick the brains of suppliers, customers, and any one else to try and get a better handle on what lies ahead in the future. Allocate a certain amount of money every year for some form of research and development. Those that plan stand to profit.

## EMPLOY INNOVATIVE ADVERTISING

Market your business in new and innovative ways, as well as using more established methods. Remember that regardless of how great your product or service is, if no one knows about it, you are doomed to fail. You cannot expect just to put up a Web site and for people just to happen across it. Internet companies have available to them a plethora of new methods to market their business. The interactivity of the Internet provides unparalleled ways to connect with current and prospective customers and learn new ways to better provide them a product or service. However, Internet companies have been so busy exploring interactive marketing methods that many have overlooked the traditional media. Television, radio, and print methods of advertising are still the most powerful methods of reaching potential customers. The Internet and technology companies that have had the most success are the ones that have engaged in innovative marketing methods through these traditional channels. Given the vast amounts of content on the Internet, banner advertisements have proved to have little value. As broadband capabilities increase, there will be much more room for creativity and integration for online marketing. We are not too far away from a time when you can be watching your favorite sitcom or sports show, click on something being worn or used, and buy it with one click. Look to be innovative in every form of advertising you do. This is how you will stand out from the pack.

## Form Your Own *Keiretsu*

Look for some way to become a part of a network of companies that work together. Internet incubators have sprung up almost overnight. With established venture capital firms providing their own network of resources and connections, incubators are trying to do the same for companies that set up shop within their confines. Incubators often provide start-ups with office space, computer equipment, back-office functions, and other important behind-the-scenes necessities so that the management team can focus on the business. Most important, they provide a community of entrepreneurs than can bounce ideas off of one another, form alliances, or just keep each other company at 11 p.m. at night. In return, they often receive a fee in addition to a certain amount of stock options or equity in the company. Incubators are becoming an excellent way for Internet entrepreneurs to get started, but there are many other ways to do it as well. Join as many networking events as possible and look to "throw business" as much as possible to your new contacts.

## Become Everybody's Partner

In the Internet revolution, having the right partnerships is key. Partnerships are one of the best ways to grow your business and make meaningful relationships with other companies. Profitable partnerships make everyone look good. Business development is an important part of every business because of its ability to help your business tap into new markets. Large Internet companies have whole groups devoted to analyzing and presenting potential partnership deals to other companies; however, you do not have to be a large company to make a deal happen. The key is finding potential partnerships that offer significant value for both sides. The Internet industry is composed of a giant network of professionals, most of whom will spend time at a number of Internet companies throughout their careers. Establish as many professional relationships with these people as possible; help them in their career and you'll make their and your company look good as well.

Always be on the lookout for new business partners, too. Whether they are strategic partnerships, joint ventures, or cobranding opportunities, partnerships help validate your business and allow it to penetrate additional target markets. Partnerships also allow your business to interact with other companies, learn new business tactics, and meet new people. In addition, you and your business will gain insight into how other companies work and their views on various industry topics. The broader your overall understanding of the industry, the better positioned you and your business are heading into the future.

Partnerships are also a way to create barriers to entry. The right types of partnerships will give you a competitive advantage in the marketplace and possibly discourage potential competitors. Partnerships are becoming imperative for every Internet company that wants to create a lasting presence and attempt to anchor itself in the vast world of the Internet.

## CREATE YOUR OWN "CLICKS AND BRICKS"

All companies wishing to thrive in the Internet revolution must combine a strong Web presence with some form of an expansive distribution set-up. Everything from customer service, merchandise returns, and building client relationships requires new, innovative methods.

Many Internet companies are turning to strategic brick-and-mortar partners that are looking for a way to tap into the Internet's power. Because so many of these companies have high overhead in terms of physical locations and employees, they want to turn them into tangible assets that can be of extreme value to Internet companies. Internet companies are growing so quickly that many are now establishing their own physical presence in certain areas. Internet cash-rich behemoths such as Amazon.com and Webvan are using their extra cash to invest in physical locations that provide some form of distribution that is not reliant on a third party. In the case of Amazon.com, it is buying huge warehouse spaces across the United States to house its products.

Another interesting distribution element is shipping. Federal Express in particular has been very active in forming relationships with numerous Internet companies to handle their expanding shipping issues. Because speed is so important, and many companies like to offer free shipping to deter customers from going to the store, many Internet companies are developing unique shipping agreements. In addition, some companies are shipping small quantities of perishable items that must be packaged in a specific way, creating a new dilemma/opportunity for both the companies and shippers. Federal Express, UPS, Airborne Express, and the United States Postal Service are all aggressively going after this business, creating a new level of interaction between Internet companies and the distributors. There will continue to be new challenges and innovative solutions for Internet companies and their distribution methods. The key is establishing a set-up that is convenient for your customers, cost-effective, and puts you at a comparative advantage over the competitors.

## CANNIBALIZE CUSTOMERS

Consumers in the online world can change their buying habits easier than ever before. Companies use an unprecedented number of special offers, discount prices, and one-time freebies to attract new consumers. With so many start-ups so well funded with millions of dollars in the bank that they are expected to spend, they are willing to take very little profit or even a loss to acquire customers. Depending on what type of product or service you are offering, you must find a way to create a sustainable competitive advantage that prevents your customers from being easily lured away.

For example, Web discount e-tailer Value America offers special Value dollars that you accrue on every purchase. These can be used to get discount on subsequent purchases. In addition, the company donates a small percentage of the order to a charity of your choice. Value America realizes that it must create unique ways to separate itself from the competition. There will almost always be someone with a lower price than what you are charging for your product or service; the key is offering something else, a value-added proposition such as great customer service or money back in their pocket, that makes the experience worthwhile for your customer.

## DON'T UNDERESTIMATE COMPETITORS

You will always have competitors, regardless of your industry. One of the first signs of naiveté to venture capitalists is when an entrepreneur sends in a business plan that describes why it has no competitors. This is impossible. In some way or another, directly or indirectly, you do have competitors, whether you realize it or not. The key is building a sustainable competitive advantage over your competitors.

Sustained competitive advantage sometimes can mean a proprietary technology, or other times it can mean forming an exclusive partnership with another company. There are many ways to create competitive advantages. It is up to you and your employees to come up with the ideas and then swiftly execute them. Having competitors is not always a bad thing. Especially in a segment of the market that is not yet developed, having multiple companies creates notice within the marketplace that there is some sort of opportunity there. This can spur business for all the companies and even create new competitors. The bottom line is that the race is always on between competitors. Who can develop the newest technology? Who can retain the best managers? Whose stock price is higher? There will always be competitors to your business, regardless of how big or small it is. Keep pushing the creative envelope to come up with innovative ways to outpace the competition and create sustainable competitive advantages.


## REMEMBER, NOTHING COMES EASY

Starting a business is never easy. No matter how great you are convinced your idea is, it will always be harder than you imagined to develop. An idea is a starting point. There will always be additions to it and modifications, and the more people exposed to it, the more people will be able to give you constructive feedback on how to execute your idea. Therefore, be realistic in everything from your financial projections to your willingness to listen to different ideas on how to develop your business. There is so much involved with turning an idea into a successful business venture. The only time it gets easier is when you add new employees, partners, and investors into the fold and you benefit from their knowledge and hard work as well.

## BE PROFITABLE (IN THE FORESEEABLE FUTURE)

A few unprofitable public Internet companies have folded, and they signal a change of times for new Internet ventures. Increasingly, it is deemed extremely important to be profitable. Be realistic; companies are built to make money. Regardless of how much your venture capitalists and bankers love you, there comes a time when you are expected to make money. Therefore, it is a good idea to become profitable as soon as possible in the coming years. If you prove your business can make money early on, investors are that much more likely to back your idea. Customer acquisition and branding are very important; however, there are other ways to put your company in the spotlight besides spending millions of dollars on a few (hopefully) well-timed advertisements. Building your team is important as well, but you can use equity compensation for this. The best way to build your company is through profits. Be ready, and become profitable as soon as possible.

## TAKE A STEP BACK

Never get so caught up in your own company that you cannot take an hour once a week to take a step back, make your own conclusions about where your market and the industry in general are heading, and reevaluate ways for your company to capitalize on changes. Remember that regardless of how successful your venture becomes, you are always susceptible to competition. On the other hand, as your business grows, you have access to existing relationships, capital, and human resources that allow you to exploit additional opportunities. A company that is not growing is dying. Take a step back once in a while and look for new ways to grow your business.

## WHAT DOES IT TAKE TO BE A SUCCESSFUL INTERNET ENTREPRENEUR?

The answer is a lot of energy, ambition, confidence, and the innovation and courage to push the limits of what already exists. Internet entrepreneurs at every stage, day in and day out, face people telling them that something will not work. The fact of the matter is that if something were so easy to do, then someone would already be doing it. Take, for example, selling wine over the Internet. It's a touchy subject that is bound to be the topic of much debate. First, selling alcohol to minors and extreme fragmentation in the distribution industry have made it a very tricky proposition to be able to sell wine over the Internet nationwide. Yet because the hurdles are so great, it makes an excellent opportunity to create an extremely defensible business once the hurdles have been overcome. The venerable VC firm Kleiner Perkins Caufield & Byers agrees, having invested millions of dollars in WineShopper.com, a Silicon Valley start-up. Although it remains to be seen how well it does, the company has assembled a stellar management team that sees these hurdles as challenges it enjoys overcoming.

Nothing is ever easy when starting any type of business. Having the right attitude is a fundamental key for a business to survive. Especially with an Internet business, where your business model may be forced to take a 180-degree turn in a matter of minutes, you must be ready both physically and mentally to handle the challenges. You have to be able to roll with the punches more than ever and be thinking in multiple directions simultaneously. The minds of Internet entrepreneurs are always working—always looking for that next big thing.

## ACQUISITION OR IPO?

The most common "desired" path for Internet entrepreneurs (especially those with VC financing) is toward an initial public offering. The valuations for public companies are almost always significantly greater than those of private companies. Therefore, the founders of a company are usually able to make the most money if their company goes public.

However, we have also seen a wave of spectacular acquisitions made during the Internet revolution. For example, Hotmail was acquired for hundreds of millions of dollars by Microsoft in 1998—not bad for a two-year-old company with no physical presence and a couple hundred employees. But Hotmail had eyeballs—millions of registered e-mail account holders for this free e-mail service represented an amazing asset for Microsoft. The name of the game is still customer acquisition, and Hotmail represented one of the largest and most marketable customer bases. This worked perfectly for Microsoft by allowing it to cross-market with the rest of the MSN community of

Web sites. Although Hotmail did not make it to the public markets, its exit strategy proved to still be fantastic.

Remember, too, that IPOs have their own headaches that acquisitions do not. There is often a holding period with the stock for a specific time period once a company has gone public. Then there are the extensive underwriting and legal fees to prepare for the offering. In addition, because an IPO is technically a funding event, you are selling equity in the company, thus further decreasing everyone's ownership position in the business. Just remember that making it to the public markets is only the first step. There must be enough interest in your stock so that there is enough volume and interest to drive the stock price higher. Underwriters are very eager these days to take companies public; however, if Wall Street does not receive it well, you could be stuck with a huge chunk of stock that you cannot unload. In addition, remember the stock price can always go down.

The bottom line is that regardless of what your exit strategy is, you must always focus on creating a sustainable competitive advantage that will allow your business to be profitable. Although it is important to keep in mind the value you are creating within the company that could be attractive to a potential suitor (be it investors or an acquirer), it is more important to be focused on the bottom line and growing your business. A profitable business always has value, even if you cannot sell it or take it public. Some entrepreneurs get too concerned with "grooming" their company to be ready for an IPO or acquisition and lose out on opportunities to grow their business. Never have your main focus on making your company "acquisition friendly." If in the end another company does not have interest in acquiring your business, you will have hit a brick wall and lost valuable time that you could have spent growing your business. Regardless of your exit strategy, keep innovating, developing, and looking for new ways to grow your business and make it more profitable. The right people will come to you when it is time to go public or sell your company.

## COMPANIES TO WATCH

Who knows if the next wave of "blue chip" companies will be businesses that have even been started yet. What will be the most successful business models of the twenty-first century? There are a few interesting companies that everyone should be watching. These include CMGI, idealab!, and Benchmark Capital, among others.

For those not familiar with these companies, CMGI began as a direct marketing firm and became one of the most prolific investors in Internet companies (owning equity stakes in companies such as Lycos, Raging Bull, and Alta Vista). Idealab! provides seed capital and guidance for entrepreneurs willing to invest their time in founder Bill Gross's ideas (companies include eToys, Tickets.com, and Citysearch). Benchmark Capital is a venture capital firm that focuses on investing in early-stage Internet companies (investors in their fund include Bill Gates, Michael Dell, the Ford Foundation, and Yale University; their big hit to date is eBay). The reason these three companies are so important to watch is that their business models are set up to acquire equity interests in a variety of companies. With their substantial capital bases and well-positioned business models, they will be "sitting pretty" to be a major voice in where the opportunities will lie in the future. Although there are numerous other venture capital and incubator companies, these three in particular may well become the new "silicon chip" companies of the next millennium.

## AND FINALLY . . .

Have fun! If nothing else, your experience as an Internet entrepreneur should be an enjoyable one. You will undoubtedly work harder than you ever have in the past; however, you should derive a sense of accomplishment and excitement that is out of this world. The majority of Internet revolutionaries never imagined the level of success they would achieve. The fact of the matter is that any one can do it, and make it big. The hardest step to take is the first. Take your knowledge of a given product, service, or industry and capitalize on a given opportunity in the marketplace. Assemble the right team and give your employees all a vested interest in the success of your venture. Create the right partnerships and establish an advisory board that will force you to look ahead and answer the tough questions.

Making it as an entrepreneur is never easy; however, the experience and potential rewards are unparalleled. Who knows when there will be such a revolutionary technology that creates such a wave of incredible opportunities again in the future. Don't wait to find out! Go for it and good luck!

# Index

# About the Authors

## JONATHAN R. ASPATORE

Jonathan R. Aspatore is the founder and managing partner of Entrepreneur Products and Services (www.spin outs.com). EPS helps existing companies exploit their business relationships, capital, and human resources in order to spin out new ventures, in any industry. Aspatore has been closely involved with the development of EPS's first portfolio company, eBrandedBooks.com, which is the only media company devoted to helping Internet and technology businesses write and self-publish easy-to-understand and entertaining books on their companies, products/services, and industries. Aspatore began his career with Morgan Stanley in New York after studying entrepreneurial management at the Wharton School of Business. He has written numerous books and articles on starting new business ventures and has contributed to various other technology and Internet-related books. For comments, questions, or inquiries about speaking opportunities, please contact him at jra@spinouts.com.

## ALICIA ABELL

Alicia Abell, an associate editor at *Washingtonian* magazine, formerly served as the online editor there. As associate editor, she writes articles on a variety of topics and is responsible for overall management of content on the *Washingtonian*'s Web site. She was a main contributor to the recently released book *The New Electronic Trader* for eBrandedBooks.com. A 1995 Dartmouth graduate, Abell taught English for a year before making the switch to journalism. She grew up in Chevy Chase, Maryland, and now resides on the other side of the river in Arlington, Virginia.